At Issue

| Drones

Other Books in the At Issue Series:

Age of Consent

Animal Experimentation

Are Abortion Rights Threatened?

Are Unions Still Relevant?

The Children of Undocumented Immigrants

Designer Babies

Do Cell Phones Cause Cancer?

Do Infectious Diseases Pose a Threat?

Extending the Human Lifespan

Has Child Behavior Worsened?

High School Dropouts

Is Foreign Aid Necessary?

Is Selling Body Parts Ethical?

Reality TV

Should Drilling Be Allowed in the Arctic National
Wildlife Refuge?

Technology and the Cloud

Teen Residential Treatment Programs

What Is the Future of the Music Industry?

What Is the Impact of Digitizing Books?

What Is the Impact of Twitter?

At Issue

|Drones

Louise Gerdes, Book Editor

GREENHAVEN PRESS
A part of Gale, Cengage Learning

Farmington Hills, Mich • San Francisco • New York • Waterville, Maine
Meriden, Conn • Mason, Ohio • Chicago

Elizabeth Des Chenes, *Director, Content Strategy*
Cynthia Sanner, *Publisher*
Douglas Dentino, *Manager, New Product*

© 2014 Greenhaven Press, a part of Gale, Cengage Learning

WCN: 01-100-101

Gale and Greenhaven Press are registered trademarks used herein under license.

For more information, contact:
Greenhaven Press
27500 Drake Rd.
Farmington Hills, MI 48331-3535
Or you can visit our Internet site at gale.cengage.com

LIBRARY OF CONGRESS CATALOGING-IN-PUBLICATION DATA

Drones / Louise Gerdes, book editor
     pages cm. -- (At issue)
     Summary: "At Issue: Drones: Books in this anthology series focus a wide range of viewpoints onto a single controversial issue, providing in-depth discussions by leading advocates, a quick grounding in the issues, and a challenge to critical thinking skills"-- Provided by publisher.
     Includes bibliographical references and index.
     ISBN 978-0-7377-6832-9 (hardback) -- ISBN 978-0-7377-6833-6 (paperback)
     1. Drone aircraft. 2. Drone aircraft--Moral and ethical aspects. I. Gerdes, Louise I., 1953-, editor.
     UG1242.D7G45 2013
     358.4--dc23
                                                            2013026135

Printed in Mexico
4 5 6 7 8 9 19 18 17 16 15

Contents

Introduction   7

1. Using Strict Standards, Targeting with   12
Drones Is Legal and Effective
Afsheen John Radsan

2. Using Drones to Fight Terrorism Has   24
Been Harmful and Ineffective
Ramesh Thakur

3. Drones Promote Terrorism   30
Ibrahim Mothana

4. How Drones Changed the Game   34
in Pakistan
Hussain Nadim

5. The Ease of Drone Warfare Raises Serious   38
Moral Questions
John Kaag and Sarah Kreps

6. Drones Should Not Be Used as an   43
International Law-Enforcement Tool
Mary Ellen O'Connell

7. CIA Drone Pilots Are Not Violating   52
International Laws of War
Charles G. Kels

8. New International Laws to Govern   56
the Use of Drones Are Needed
America Magazine

9. How Drones Are Used to Fight Terrorism   60
Requires Public Debate
Ben Iannotta

10. The Domestic Use of Drones Poses   63
    Serious Threats to Civil Liberties
    John W. Whitehead

11. Drone, Sweet Drone   68
    Micah Zenko

12. Drones Are Effective for Border Security   74
    and Disaster Assistance
    Michael C. Kostelnik

13. The Ability of Drones to Secure America's   84
    Borders Remains Unproven
    Brian Bennett

14. Drones Are an Effective Environmental   89
    Protection Tool
    Denis D. Gray

15. A Drone Industry Code of Conduct Is   94
    Inadequate to Protect Americans
    Peter W. Singer and Jeffrey Lin

16. Legal Safeguards Are Needed to Protect   100
    Against Domestic Use of Drones
    Amie Stepanovich

Organizations to Contact   111

Bibliography   116

Index   120

Introduction

Unmanned aerial vehicles, commonly referred to as drones, serve many roles in domestic, military, and Central Intelligence Agency (CIA) operations. Indeed, the controversies surrounding drones are closely related to how they are used by the government. According to military historians, the original role for drones was to conduct surveillance in hostile territory without risking a pilot's life. When in 1960 Francis Gary Powers and his U-2 spy plane were shot down over the Soviet Union,[1] the United States Air Force (USAF) launched a classified program to develop unmanned surveillance aircraft. Although the US military would not comment on Communist Chinese claims that the United States used drones during the Vietnam conflict, military leaders later officially confirmed their use. USAF General George S. Brown explained in 1972, "The only reason we need [UAVs] is that we don't want to needlessly expend the man in the cockpit."[2] General John C. Meyer, then commander in chief of the Strategic Air Command, that same year agreed: "We let the drone do the high-risk flying. . . . They save lives!"[3]

The military continues to use drones for surveillance. In fact, drones provided surveillance video prior to the US Navy SEAL attack that killed Osama bin Laden, on May 2, 2011. Reflecting their ability to see from afar or go unnoticed, surveillance drones are given names such as Wasp, Gnat, Dragon Eye, and Global Hawk. The names of drones that serve a more deadly purpose have equally reflective names. Predator and

1. Francis Gary Powers was convicted of espionage by the Soviet judicial system and sentenced to three years imprisonment and seven years of hard labor. However, he served a little less than two years, when he was traded for the Soviet spy Colonel Rudolf Ivanovich Abel. This incident created a culture of mistrust that some claim culminated in the Cuban Missile Crisis of 1962.
2. As quoted in William Wagner, *Lightning Bugs and Other Reconnaissance Drones*, Fallbrook, CA: Armed Forces Journal, 1982.
3. *Ibid.*

Reaper drones are hunters and killers. The USAF Predator, originally designed to carry cameras and sensors to conduct reconnaissance, was later upgraded to fire Hellfire missiles.[4] Following the terrorist attacks of September 11, 2001, the Predator became the primary aircraft used during military and CIA operations in Afghanistan and the tribal areas of Pakistan where many terrorists hide. The Reaper, the prototype of which is known by its manufacturer, General Atomics, as Predator B, is larger, faster, and more capable. It can carry more ordnance and has more advanced surveillance sensors. Its use is primarily military but versions of the Reaper have been used by NASA for research and to map the 2007 wildfires in California. The infrared sensors of another version of the Reaper provide the US Customs and Border Protection (CBP) optimal views of activity on the nation's borders. These versions, however, have less deadly names. The CBP version is called Guardian and the NASA version, Ikhana, which in the language of the Native American Choctaw nation means "intelligent."

Although some question the domestic use of surveillance drones, few question their use in the military. However, when drones are used as weapons of war, even some in the military express concern over their impact. Andrew Exum, a former Army Ranger and coauthor of a study on counter-insurgency warfare, maintains, "there's something about pilotless drones that doesn't strike me as an honorable way of warfare."[5] Although Exum helped design the military's doctrine for using unmanned drones, he suggests, "There's something important about putting your own sons and daughters at risk when you choose to wage war as a nation. We risk losing that flesh-and-

4. The Hellfire missile is a proven air-to-surface tactical missile in use since the mid-1980s. The military developed the missile primarily to defeat armored vehicles. The Hellfire is the primary precision weapon used by the US armed forces and many other nations.

5. As quoted in Jane Mayer, "The Predator War," *New Yorker*, October 26, 2009.

blood investment if we go too far down this road."[6] Although military leaders try to balance the lifesaving benefits and ethical challenges of drone warfare, the military use of drones remains controversial.

The most contentious use of drones, however, is the targeted killing of suspected terrorists by the CIA. Those critical of the use of drones to target terrorists oppose their use for several reasons. Some argue that the collateral damage to civilians is too great. Reports vary over the actual numbers, but according to the New America Foundation, a Washington, DC, think tank, as many as a third of the casualties of drone strikes between 2004 and 2008 were civilians. Others argue that such attacks violate the sovereignty of nations not at war with the United States. In truth, Pakistan, the location of a majority of drone strikes, is one of America's greatest allies in the fight against terrorism. Opponents believe that drone attacks increase anti-Americanism in Pakistan and in turn create future terrorists. Although the Pakistani government generally condones strikes designed to kill the terrorists living in its tribal regions, the collateral damage has led some Pakistani leaders to oppose the US drone policy.

Moreover, some drone opponents claim, CIA drones are piloted by civilians. Since CIA drone pilots are not soldiers, CIA drone strikes are illegal, these commentators claim. Opponents label these strikes extrajudicial killings—executions conducted without the due process of law. Opposition increased when in Yemen, on September 30, 2011, CIA drone strikes killed two al Qaeda commanders who were also Americans. Indeed, following these attacks, US senator Ron Wyden led a campaign to gain access to the decision-making process behind these killings and called for increasing transparency of CIA drone strikes. In fact, Wyden and others in Congress held up the congressional hearings to confirm the new CIA director, John Brennan, in order to pressure the Obama adminis-

6. *Ibid.*

tration to provide access to classified presidential memos on drone strikes and to hold the CIA accountable. According to Wyden, "I think every American has the right to know when their government believes it has the right to kill them."[7]

Drone strike supporters, on the other hand, believe the strikes are both legal and necessary. In truth, a February 2012 *Washington Post*–ABC News poll revealed that 83 percent of Americans approve of the Obama administration's drone policy, and 65 percent approve of using drones to target US citizens abroad. Attorney General Eric Holder, in a March 5, 2012, speech at Northwestern University Law School, maintained, "The unfortunate reality is that our nation will likely continue to face terrorist threats that—at times—originate with our own citizens. When such individuals take up arms against this country—and join Al Qaeda in plotting attacks designed to kill their fellow Americans . . . we must take steps to stop them—in full accordance with the Constitution."[8] Drone advocates often argue that the modern war on terror requires a broader view of warfare. In a September 16, 2011, speech at Harvard Law School, John O. Brennan asserted, "The United States does not view our authority to use military force against Al Qaeda as being restricted to 'hot' battlefields like Afghanistan."[9] Attorney General Holder agrees: "In this hour of danger, we simply cannot afford to wait until deadly plans are carried out. This is an indicator of our times—not a departure from our laws and our values."[10]

Commentators continue to contest whether the use of drones is a necessary counterterrorism tool or whether targeted drone strikes are instead a form of extrajudicial killing that involves unnecessary collateral damage. The authors of

---

7. As quoted in Tal Kopan, "Still 'Long Way to Go' Getting Answers on Drone Memos," *Politico*, March 13, 2013. http://www.politico.com/blogs/under-the-radar/2013/03/wyden-still-long-way-to-go-getting-answers-on-drone-159211.html.

8. Eric Holder, speech at Northwestern University Law School, March 5, 2012.

9. John O. Brennan, speech at Harvard Law School, September 16, 2011.

10. Holder, *op. cit.*

the viewpoints in *At Issue: Drones* explore these and other issues in the drone debate. Efforts to increase the transparency of US drone policy continue as do requests to further expand the use of drones. According to a 2012 Pentagon report, drones remain a key component of the military's counterterrorism force. The report called for a 30 percent increase in the Department of Defense's drone fleet. In addition, in 2012, the Federal Aviation Administration issued as many as 285 permits to test drone use in American airspace. Some analysts assert that the revolution in unmanned aviation will only increase in scope and sophistication. How policy makers respond to the legal and ethical challenges posed by drones remains to be seen.

1

Using Strict Standards, Targeting with Drones Is Legal and Effective

Afsheen John Radsan

Afsheen John Radsan, law professor at William Mitchell College of Law, was assistant general counsel at the Central Intelligence Agency from 2002 to 2004.

Terrorists are in essence armed combatants at war with the United States. Thus, using drones to target and kill them is legal according to international laws that govern warfare. However, because US drone pilots do not face the same risks as soldiers in the battlefield, they must meet strict standards of certainty that those targeted are indeed terrorists. In addition, to avoid abuses and ensure accountability, drone strikes should be subject to oversight. Such precautions are necessary so that drone warfare meets the guidelines of armed conflict under international law. In the end, targeted killing with drones is effective if it is proportionate—the impact on the enemy is much greater than any collateral damage.

". . . [CIA] sharpshooters killed eight people suspected of being militants of the Taliban and Al Qaeda . . . in a compound that was said to be used for terrorist training. Then, the job in North Waziristan [Pakistan] done, the CIA officers could head home from the agency's Langley, Va., headquarters, facing only the hazards of the area's famously

Afsheen John Radsan, "Loftier Standards for the CIA's Remote-Control Killing," Statement for the House Subcommittee on National Security & Foreign Affairs," April 28, 2010.

snarled suburban traffic."—Scott Shane, "C.I.A. to Expand Use of Drones in Pakistan," *New York Times*, December 3, 2009.

The Bush administration started using drones to target and kill leaders of al Qaeda and the Taliban. Since President Obama has embraced this targeted killing, the number of strikes has soared. The Obama administration has even added an American citizen who lives in Yemen—Anwar al-Awlaki—to the list of persons targeted for death.

Killer drones are the future of warfare. The drone's extraordinary capabilities have expanded our government's range for finding, tracking, and destroying human targets. As a result, targeted killing—whether by the CIA or anyone else—is controversial. Proponents contend it is legal to use armed drones in self-defense or as part of an armed conflict under international humanitarian law (IHL). Critics decry targeted killing as extra-judicial assassination.

Shaping Limits and Standards

I believe IHL covers the CIA's drone campaign, particularly in parts of Pakistan. The Obama administration, of course, shares this belief. I also believe that operational parts of al Qaeda and the Taliban are civilians "directly participating in hostilities." Until they renounce violence, they are functional combatants, subjecting them to American targeting under the law. I am confident a consensus will emerge that, under some circumstances, targeted killing of suspected terrorists is legal. Ahead of that consensus, I try to shape specific limits on the level of certainty for targeting and on the standard for independent review of strikes.

I note but do not examine the implications of having a civilian agency involved in lethal action. Some say the Defense Department should have an exclusive role in America's targeted killing. But this is not the first time the CIA has been asked to kill, and I assume the CIA will continue to take a piece of the high-profile action on the drone. While CIA officers are unlikely to wear uniforms and to follow other military formalities, they take it for granted, whether engaged in intelligence gathering or in covert action, that they will not be treated as privileged belligerents (POWs) if al Qaeda captures them. They have more basic concerns.

The [CIA] may strike only if it is satisfied beyond a reasonable doubt that its target is a functional combatant of al Qaeda or a similar terrorist group.

Several IHL principles should moderate the CIA's targeted killing. (Similar principles also apply if the legal justification is self-defense separate from an armed conflict.) First, IHL requires *distinction*, separating combatants from civilians and precluding the targeting of peaceful civilians. Second, IHL insists that *military necessity* justify all attacks: an attack should be reasonably expected to create a concrete and direct military advantage. Third, IHL requires *proportionality*: attacks must not cause excessive collateral damage. To give effect to these principles, IHL also speaks of *precaution*, which requires all feasible measures to minimize harm to peaceful civilians and property.

Controlling the CIA's Drones

The CIA should have standards for identifying targets and for carrying out strikes. Depending on one's perspective, these controls can be viewed as developing general IHL principles or as departing from rules that apply in traditional armed conflicts.

First, the agency should impose a very high standard in identifying targets. Except in extraordinary circumstances, the agency may strike only if it is satisfied beyond a reasonable doubt that its target is a functional combatant of al Qaeda or a similar terrorist group. Those who believe that reasonable doubt carries too much baggage from criminal law or that it inappropriately mixes criminal justice with war should substitute another label for a very high level of certainty. My idea, however labeled, is for the drone operator to be really sure before pulling the trigger. Drone strikes, in effect, are executions without any realistic chance for appeal to the courts through *habeas corpus* or other procedures.

Second, to ensure the inter-related goals of accuracy, legality, and accountability, all CIA targeted killings should be subject to independent review by the CIA's Inspector General that is as public as national security permits.

Distinction Beyond Reasonable Doubt. Imagine two American fighters. A Marine is on the ground in the Helmand province of Afghanistan while a drone pilot is in the United States, many miles away from the action. These two Americans, soldier and pilot, are both on the watch for bad guys. The two Americans try their best to follow the rules—which include IHL and any rules of engagement (ROEs) produced back at the Pentagon and the CIA.

The law expects much more from the drone pilot than from the soldier on the ground.

The soldier on the ground must often make quick decisions based on inadequate information. The enemy's practice of hiding among peaceful civilians makes it quite difficult for him to determine who is a legal target—especially when civilians carry weapons for protection from thieves, bandits, and insurgents. So what does the Marine do about another man walking down the street with an AK-47? "When in doubt," one not so imaginary Marine says about this situation, "empty the magazine."[1] This response is wrong as a matter of law, but

---

1. This phrase, "when in doubt, empty the magazine," refers to a policy that when a soldier is unsure of the risk posed by possible combatants, the best strategy is to disable or kill them.

it highlights circumstances that must be considered in any realistic assessment of the soldier's legal obligations.

A drone pilot—supplied with multiple sources of intelligence, armed with the latest technology, and located thousands of miles from the enemy—must be more circumspect. Her instructions to kill are based on a deliberative process. Once the drone is in place, the pilot and a team of analysts may be able to spend hours studying the ground to confirm the target's identity.

Because the solider and the pilot operate in different circumstances, the law does not expect the same from them. The law expects much more from the drone pilot than from the soldier on the ground. Because precise technology increases the CIA's ability to control its force, IHL imposes a corresponding duty to do so.

A High Level of Certainty

But just telling the drone pilot that she must be more careful with her missiles than the soldier must with his gun is not enough. A more precise instruction is necessary: targeted killing by drone may go forward only where it is clear beyond reasonable doubt that the target is legitimate according to the facts and the law. Before firing the missile, the drone pilot (or whoever else gives the order to kill) should be quite certain that the target functions as a member of al Qaeda who plans, commands, or carries out attacks.

A high level of certainty is consistent with America's official stance. In a public defense of drone attacks, the State Department's legal adviser, Harold Koh, remarked:

> In U.S. operations against al Qaeda and its associated forces—including lethal operations conducted with the use of unmanned aerial vehicles—*great care* is taken to adhere to these principles [of distinction and proportionality] in

both planning and execution, to ensure that *only legitimate objectives are targeted* and that collateral damage is kept to a minimum.

Strictly speaking, Koh's remarks do not address the CIA. But his speech was obviously intended to reassure an uncertain audience about CIA activities. In line with Koh's comments, recall the general IHL rule that targeting should be reasonable based on the circumstances. So my proposal for a high level of certainty in CIA targeting is a straightforward application of IHL's rule of reason based on specific facts. Factored into the equation are the multiple sources of intelligence, the time for deliberation, and the relative safety of the drone pilot.

The principle of military necessity reinforces my conclusion. This principle condemns an attack if it will cause suffering not reasonably necessary to achieve a concrete and direct military advantage. With drones, however, force protection is largely irrelevant because the air vessels are unmanned. Therefore, unless the drones are seen as part of a larger American military force, targeted killing by this new weapon satisfies military necessity only if it causes sufficient harm to the enemy—and it does not create a disproportionate number of new recruits for al Qaeda and the Taliban.

There are, of course, exceptions to my general rule for CIA targeting. I summarize these exceptions under the label of extraordinary circumstances. The target, for example, may play an irreplaceable role in al Qaeda. A drone operator may see a person on the screen who is probably Bin Laden—but not Bin Laden beyond any doubt. Even so, the military advantage of killing Bin Laden,[2] compared to a mid-level terrorist, may justify the additional risk of mistakenly harming a peaceful civilian. Targeting the man at the top, it turns out, does not have to be as certain. Yet the relevant agency (whether the CIA or

2. On May 2, 2011, Osama bin Laden was shot and killed inside a private residential compound in Pakistan by members of the US Naval Special Warfare Development Group and Central Intelligence Agency operatives in a covert operation ordered by President Barack Obama.

the Air Force) bears the burden of justifying any departure from the default rule of heightened certainty. This burden, of course, is met within the internal due process of the Executive branch, not in any external due process before a court.

For CIA drone strikes, the interest in accountability is acute given the veil of secrecy over CIA activities and the specter that targeted killing could become distorted into random acts of murder.

Precaution and Independent, Ex Post Review. IHL insists that attackers take all feasible measures to get things right. Despite the agency's reputation for playing fast and loose with the law, CIA officials must be acutely aware that, for many observers, targeted killings come close to prohibited assassinations. To stay safe, CIA officials seek both political and legal cover. From past lessons on controversial programs, CIA officials have learned to obtain presidential authorization in writing, to brief the oversight committees, and to obtain legal opinions. So, I bet President Obama has blessed the CIA drone strikes; the oversight committees have not been kept in the dark; the CIA has developed internal procedures; and the agency has presented these procedures to the Justice Department's Office of Legal Counsel for approval.

Because the concept of precaution is so vague, the procedures to fulfill this IHL duty might reasonably take many forms. If experience from the classified setting shows a particular set of procedures results in too much collateral damage, then the CIA must adopt stricter procedures. This is a "feedback loop" the Defense Department is accustomed to in its "after-action" studies from prior bombing campaigns. The CIA must do the same.

Whatever the CIA's standards and procedures, they are much more likely to be enforced when the decision-maker is required to explain her decision to an independent authority at a later time. For CIA drone strikes, the interest in accountability is acute given the veil of secrecy over CIA activities and the specter that targeted killing could become distorted into random acts of murder. At the same time, the CIA has an interest in protecting sources and methods for national security. The question, in reconciling democracy with secrecy, is what sort of accountability best balances these interests.

Distinguishing the Military Model

Answering that question requires a leap from IHL. The military model is distinct for several reasons: (a) a traditional armed conflict requires hundreds of people to make decisions, often under stress, fatigue, and danger; (b) many decisions are straightforward because the enemy is easy to identify (*e.g.*, it is obviously legal for a solider to shoot at an enemy tank with no civilians near it); (c) much of the information needed to second-guess these decisions is covered in the rubble of war; and (d) the self-evident boundaries to the conflict allay concerns that supposed combatants will be killed anywhere in the world in the name of national security.

To select a target, the agency [CIA] must seek and assess all available intelligence.

The CIA's drone campaign, to repeat, differs from traditional armed conflict. First, the limited number of strikes means it is practicable to subject every strike to independent investigation. Second, by definition, all strikes have lethal consequences, and the danger from a misfired missile is much higher than the danger from a misfired pistol. Third, the information to evaluate these strikes stays available: video, audio, cables, and other documents. All this information provides for meaningful *ex post* review.

Fourth, and most important, since the CIA is given leeway to operate in the shadows, a countervailing check is needed.

Even if the Obama administration is carrying out targeted killing accurately and wisely, the potential for abuse stays with us. How many countries are within the killing field? How many more countries are to come? Will Predators ever be used on American territory? As a check against abuses, IHL requires feasible precautions.

Finding the Right Balance

Who should conduct this review of drone strikes? And what should the scope of review be? The reviewing entity should not substitute its judgment, but should patrol against clearly unreasonable judgments. It is review, not micro-management. For the right balance, American administrative law is useful.

Administrative law tries both to ensure that an agency follows the law and to respect the agency's zone for reasonable discretion. The doctrine of "reasoned decision-making," in particular, provides a template for this delicate balance. Using this template, a court examines whether an agency made its decision based on all "relevant factors" or whether the agency made a "clear error of judgment." We can also call this examination the "hard-look." Hard-look tries to learn what an agency *actually* considered in making its decision. The court, in this sort of review, looks for an agency's contemporaneous explanation of its action. An agency is thus prevented from using post-hoc rationalizations for decisions reached on less defensible grounds.

On CIA drone strikes, the hard-look is a good fit, particularly on target selection done before an attack. To select a target, the agency must seek and assess all available intelligence. This assessment should be laid out in exhaustive findings that include: (a) grounds for concluding the target is a functional combatant; (b) any grounds for doubting this status; (c) whether killing the target creates a concrete and direct military advantage; (d) whether that advantage is sufficient to justify any risk of collateral damage, and if so, how much; and

(e) any military or political disadvantages that might result from a strike. The hard-look insists that the agency memorialize its decision-making process; at the same time, it applies a deferential standard of clear error to outcomes in the field of armed conflict.

On the first question of *who* should conduct this sort of review, I propose the CIA's IG [Inspector General]. As appropriate, the IG could recommend internal discipline, compensation to unwarranted victims of a strike, or, in an extreme case of abuse, referral to the Justice Department for criminal proceedings. The IG should also be involved in reviewing the CIA's procedures on target selection and execution of attacks. The IG's due process, so to speak, substitutes for what otherwise comes from the courts. To enhance accountability, IG reports could be made public. The CIA could thus acknowledge a general role in drone strikes without mentioning particular countries. This would balance the interests of accountability against the CIA's common need to keep secret the role of foreign governments in assisting American intelligence.

One Process for All

The government's power to kill must be carefully controlled—or it could turn into a tyranny worse than terrorism. The traditional control, however, does not work for targeted killing; only the fanciful would propose a full judicial trial in which the government and the suspected terrorist make opening statements, admit evidence, and argue the suspect's fate to the jury. So a new model must be developed which recognizes that fighting terrorism is as much war as it is law enforcement. For that reason, I tend to propose hybrids and transplants.

IHL does not consider citizenship in distinguishing combatants from civilians. In traditional conflicts, the United States has had citizens switch to the other side. Switched, they become targets just like foreign combatants. Nonetheless, news that the Obama administration placed at least one American citizen on a hit list caused some outrage. The outrage, it seems, stems from either a mistaken intuition or a flawed legal objection.

If the controls are not good enough for killing Americans, then they are not good enough for killing Pakistanis, Afghans, or Yemenis.

The intuition is that there is something especially wrong about the American government killing Americans. People, no doubt, treat members of their own group better than outsiders; to kill someone, it helps to label him an "outsider." Yet, at a higher morality, the American government, independent of other factors, should not feel freer to kill non-Americans. The flip-side, morally speaking, is that the American government has just as much standing to kill Americans as non-Americans.

Answering Legal Objections

The legal objection is that killing an American by drone strike violates due process under the United States Constitution. This objection depends on two misplaced premises. The first is that extraterritorial actions which the American government takes against non-citizens do not implicate due process. I argued in an earlier piece on targeted killing that the Supreme Court's decision in *Boumediene v. Bush* suggests that this premise is mistaken. *Boumediene* leads to the conclusion that the United States Constitution applies overseas where it is practicable. At bottom, the right to due process is the right to fair and reasonable procedures. For CIA activities, the due process might come from some combination of CIA lawyers, the Inspector General, and the review boards within the CIA's clandestine service.

The second premise is that due process requires a judicial trial before the United States may kill one of its own citizens.

In a law-enforcement context, the trial requirement holds true except where the target poses an immediate and severe threat. It does not hold true, however, under IHL. During World War II, for instance, it was legal for American soldiers—without a judicial trial—to fire on American citizens who fought for the Nazis.

Since World War II, the American courts have developed various models of due process: a due process of prisons; a due process for discipline in schools; and a due process for detaining American citizens as enemy combatants. Our nation is now developing a due process for targeted killing by drone. If non-American lives are just as important as American lives, then one model of due process (or "precaution" to use an IHL term), should apply across the board. In negative terms, if the controls are not good enough for killing Americans, then they are not good enough for killing Pakistanis, Afghans, or Yemenis.

International humanitarian law can be developed into specific regulations for the CIA's targeted killing. Accordingly, the drone operator must be sure beyond a reasonable doubt that the trigger is being pulled on a functional enemy combatant. In addition, she must conclude that the requirements of military necessity and proportionality have been met. Afterward, the CIA's Inspector General must review each CIA drone strike, including the agency's compliance with a checklist of standards and procedures.

A program that establishes a very high certainty for targeting as well as a hard-look after each strike will be fair and reasonable whether the people in the cross-hairs are Americans or citizens from other countries. In the language of IHL, these are feasible precautions for the remote-control weapons of the new century.

2

Using Drones to Fight Terrorism Has Been Harmful and Ineffective

Ramesh Thakur

Ramesh Thakur, public policy professor at Australian National University and the Institute for Ethics, Governance and Law, Griffith University, is editor-in-chief of Global Governance, *a journal that explores the processes of international cooperation and multilateralism.*

Although using drones to target terrorists is cheaper and poses less risk to US soldiers, studies show that drone strikes have killed few high-level terrorist leaders. Moreover, the president of the United States should not have the power to kill others without judicial or independent review. In fact, according to some legal experts, the use of drones to kill terrorists undermines international law. Indeed, the use of drones to target terrorists in other countries violates the sovereignty of those nations. Although drones reduce the cost of war, they may lead to an increase in their use when little evidence demonstrates that they make Americans safer.

Over the weekend, defying death threats from the militants whose writ is law in the region, former cricketer and presently Pakistan's most popular political leader Imran Khan led but had to abort a march into the country's northwestern tribal areas to protest against U.S. drone strikes that have killed between 2,000–3,000 people. The buzz of the U.S. fleet of Predator and Reaper drones that at any moment can let loose their deadly arsenal of Hellfire missiles is a familiar terror in the sky for the people of Waziristan.

We live in an age of technological warfare coexisting uneasily alongside the use of machetes on an industrial scale in Rwanda in 1994 and commercial aircraft as lethally effective delivery systems on Sept. 11, 2001. Its high-tech arsenal enables the U.S. to project military power to the remotest corners of the world, distancing combat forces from the victims of their firepower. The U.S. has more than 7,000 drones today compared to 50 just a decade ago. By the end of next year [2013] there will be more U.S. Air Force personnel operating drones than flying planes.

The Allure of Drones

Such technological prowess holds the seductive allure of war and morality on the cheap.

But is it? Moral deliberations and legal accountability rooted in social purposes cannot be outsourced to robots and machines.

Drones have greater endurance, cost less, reduce the risk to U.S. soldiers to zero, and kill fewer innocent civilians. They can be flown for long hours over treacherous, inhospitable terrain and vast distances. Many al-Qaida and Taliban commanders, it is claimed, have been killed, captured, dispersed and driven deep underground, their leadership decapitated and global networks disrupted, thereby preventing numerous terrorist and insurgent attacks.

But according to the New American Foundation's data, since 2004, only 49 high-value militant leaders have been killed in strikes (accounting for just 2 percent of all drone killings). The rest have been largely low-level combatants.

Extrajudicial Killing

Over 80 percent of deaths by drones have come under U.S. President Barack Obama. He presides over the regular Tuesday counterterrorism meeting in the White House and signs off personally on additions to the kill list. His self-belief betrays a supreme self-confidence bordering on moral-intellectual arrogance (a trait that tripped him up badly in the first presidential debate). He wields the power of life and death over citizens and foreigners without judicial review or independent accountability. A *Daily Mail* columnist dubs him the "Lord High Executioner."

There are numerous legal, moral and strategic problems with the use of drones to kill the enemy.

What is the moral distinction between war, pre-emptive execution by bureaucratic decisions made in secret and murder? Does targeted killing represent an extraterritorial extension of the normative authority of the state to cover gaps in the existing legal order, or is it a covert attempt to breach the limits of the legal competence of a state in foreign jurisdictions?

Top legal experts who had eloquently condemned the torture practices under U.S. President George W. Bush have serially defended the Obama targeted killings as consistent with applicable laws of war. U.S. Attorney General Eric Holder argues that the U.S. Constitution "guarantees due process, not judicial process" for U.S. citizens. That requirement is satisfied by the conditions attached to putting someone on the kill list: The person must be a senior operational leader of al-Qaida or associated forces; capture is not feasible; and the operation is conducted in conformity with applicable laws of war principles.

Undermining the Rule of Law

There are numerous legal, moral and strategic problems with the use of drones to kill the enemy. An exhaustive new study by the law schools of Stanford and New York universities concludes that they have traumatized and terrorized an entire population. They have undermined respect for the rule of law and international legal protection. They set dangerous precedents for facilitating the recourse to lethal force around the world even as lethal drone technologies are being developed by several countries and export control barriers are softening. More than 50 countries (and counting) now have the use of drones. On Sunday, Israel shot down an unarmed and unidentified drone that entered its airspace from the Mediterranean.

> *There is no clear evidence that [drones] have made America safer overall. They expand the pool of angry and twisted young men for recruitment into the ranks of jihadists.*

They violate the sovereignty of Pakistan, a country with which the U.S. is not at war. They also violate the requirements of distinction, proportionality, humanity and military necessity under international humanitarian law. Strikes on mosques, funerals, schools and meetings of elders; signature strikes based not on individually identified targets but on behavior patterns (is a group of young men, in a country where every adult male has a beard and carries a gun, performing jumping jacks engaged in innocent fun of youth or engaged in terrorist training?); and strikes on rescuers and first responders are particularly troubling. The classification of all military-age males as combatants, based on the logic of guilt-by-association, reinforces concerns on proportionality.

U.N. special rapporteurs,[1] too, have argued that extrajudicial killings using drones pose a challenge to international law, may constitute war crimes and risk developing a "PlayStation mentality" to killing. Acts of extrajudicial assassination may also be illegal under U.S. domestic law.

The convenience of drones produces the perverse incentive of lowering the threshold of the resort to lethal violence by reducing the risks and costs of war. Because political leaders do not have to agonize over putting sons and daughters in harm's way, they can make decisions on war and peace without the earlier heavy heart.

Increasing Hatred of the United States

Yet there is no clear evidence that they have made America safer overall. They expand the pool of angry and twisted young men for recruitment into the ranks of jihadists. Faisal Shahzad, the failed Times Square bomber of May 2010, when asked about potential innocent victims of his plot, replied: "U.S. drone strikes don't see children, they don't see anybody. They kill women, children; they kill everybody." Drones have made the U.S. more hated than India in Pakistan.

Another cost is the deepening antagonism of several Western as well as Islamic peoples toward the U.S. Public opinion polls show that most Americans support but most others oppose drone strikes, often by substantial margins. Being unilateral, they reinforce the widespread perception of the U.S. as a self-concerned state that acts without consideration for others.

The moral qualms over a president claiming the right to kill foreign and U.S. citizens based on a secret process with no contestability, checks and balances have grown and deepened. The inflection point of diminishing utility and returns has

---

1. Rapporteur is a French-derived word for an investigator who reports to a deliberative body. United Nations special rapporteurs are people who receive a specific mandate from a body such as the United Nations Human Rights Council to investigate possible human rights abuses.

been reached. The U.S. risks becoming world leader in killing people with no connection to 9/11, to al-Qaida or to any other terrorist group. On the balance of consequences test, drone strikes are doing more harm than good.

3

Drones Promote Terrorism

Ibrahim Mothana

Ibrahim Mothana is a writer and community activist in Yemen, as well as the cofounder of the Watan party, which advocates individual initiative and social responsibility.

Drone attacks targeting terrorists that also result in the death of innocent civilians risk turning potential allies into enemies. Indeed, drone strikes promote terrorism by encouraging angry citizens to join militant groups, not because they support a radical ideology but out of a desire for revenge. Rather than resort to force, the better counterterrorism strategy is to understand what drives people to extreme ideologies. Building better economic and social relations with the people of these nations will encourage them to work with the United States to eliminate radical Islamic fundamentalism.

"Dear Obama, when a U.S. drone missile kills a child in Yemen, the father will go to war with you, guaranteed. Nothing to do with Al Qaeda," a Yemeni lawyer warned on Twitter last month [May 2012]. President [Barack] Obama should keep this message in mind before ordering more drone strikes like Wednesday's, which local officials say killed 27 people, or the May 15 strike that killed at least eight Yemeni civilians.

Alienating Allies

Drone strikes are causing more and more Yemenis to hate America and join radical militants; they are not driven by ideology but rather by a sense of revenge and despair. Robert

Ibrahim Mothana, "How Drones Help Al Qaeda," *New York Times*, June 13, 2012.

Grenier, the former head of the C.I.A.'s counterterrorism center, has warned that the American drone program in Yemen risks turning the country into a safe haven for Al Qaeda like the tribal areas of Pakistan—"the Arabian equivalent of Waziristan."[1]

Anti-Americanism is far less prevalent in Yemen than in Pakistan. But rather than winning the hearts and minds of Yemeni civilians, America is alienating them by killing their relatives and friends. Indeed, the drone program is leading to the Talibanization[2] of vast tribal areas and the radicalization of people who could otherwise be America's allies in the fight against terrorism in Yemen.

The increasing civilian toll of drone strikes is turning the apathy of tribal factions into anger.

The first known drone strike in Yemen to be authorized by Mr. Obama, in late 2009, left 14 women and 21 children dead in the southern town of al-Majala, according to a parliamentary report. Only one of the dozens killed was identified as having strong Qaeda connections.

Misleading intelligence has also led to disastrous strikes with major political and economic consequences. An American drone strike in May 2010 killed Jabir al-Shabwani, a prominent sheik and the deputy governor of Marib Province. The strike had dire repercussions for Yemen's economy. The slain sheik's tribe attacked the country's main pipeline in revenge. With 70 percent of the country's budget dependent on oil exports, Yemen lost over $1 billion. This strike also erased

1. Waziristan is a mountainous tribal region in northwest Pakistan, separated from the nation's core provinces, to which many terrorists have fled.
2. Talibanization is the process of converting a government or culture to the fundamentalist Islamic teachings of the Taliban, a Muslim group that controlled much of Afghanistan from 1995 until US military intervention in 2001.

years of progress and trust-building with tribes who considered it a betrayal given their role in fighting Al Qaeda in their areas.

Yemeni tribes are generally quite pragmatic and are by no means a default option for radical religious groups seeking a safe haven. However, the increasing civilian toll of drone strikes is turning the apathy of tribal factions into anger.

Recruiting Terrorists

The strikes have created an opportunity for terrorist groups like Al Qaeda in the Arabian Peninsula [AQAP] and Ansar al-Sharia to recruit fighters from tribes who have suffered casualties, especially in Yemen's south, where mounting grievances since the 1994 civil war have driven a strong secessionist movement.

There may be short-term military gains from killing militant leaders in these strikes, but they are minuscule compared with the long-term damage the drone program is causing.

Unlike Al Qaeda in Iraq, A.Q.A.P. has worked on gaining the support of local communities by compromising on some of their strict religious laws and offering basic services, electricity and gas to villagers in the areas they control. Furthermore, Iran has seized this chance to gain more influence among the disgruntled population in Yemen's south.

And the situation is quite likely to get worse now that Washington has broadened its rules of engagement to allow so-called signature strikes, when surveillance data suggest a terrorist leader may be nearby but the identities of all others targeted is not known. Such loose rules risk redefining "militants" as any military-age males seen in a strike zone.

Certainly, there may be short-term military gains from killing militant leaders in these strikes, but they are minuscule compared with the long-term damage the drone program is causing. A new generation of leaders is spontaneously emerging in furious retaliation to attacks on their territories and tribes.

This is why A.Q.A.P. is much stronger in Yemen today than it was a few years ago. In 2009, A.Q.A.P. had only a few hundred members and controlled no territory; today it has, along with Ansar al-Sharia, at least 1,000 members and controls substantial amounts of territory.

Overlooking the Real Drivers of Extremism

Yemenis are the ones who suffer the most from the presence of Al Qaeda, and getting rid of this plague is a priority for the majority of Yemen's population. But there is no shortcut in dealing with it. Overlooking the real drivers of extremism and focusing solely on tackling their security symptoms with brutal force will make the situation worse.

Only a long-term approach based on building relations with local communities, dealing with the economic and social drivers of extremism, and cooperating with tribes and Yemen's army will eradicate the threat of Islamic radicalism.

Unfortunately, liberal voices in the United States are largely ignoring, if not condoning, civilian deaths and extrajudicial killings in Yemen—including the assassination of three American citizens in September 2011, including a 16-year-old. During George W. Bush's presidency, the rage would have been tremendous. But today there is little outcry, even though what is happening is in many ways an escalation of Mr. Bush's policies.

Defenders of human rights must speak out. America's counterterrorism policy here is not only making Yemen less safe by strengthening support for A.Q.A.P., but it could also ultimately endanger the United States and the entire world.

4

How Drones Changed the Game in Pakistan

Hussain Nadim

Hussain Nadim is a visiting scholar at the Woodrow Wilson Center, a think tank established by an act of Congress in 1968 to memorialize the twenty-eighth US president and his goal to build a bridge between the worlds of academia and public policy, and to inform and develop solutions to the nation's problems and challenges.

Claims that drone strikes actually promote terrorism by creating more terrorists are inaccurate. In truth, people in tribal areas of nations such as Pakistan want to flush the terrorists out of their communities, and support for drone strikes is widespread in the Pakistani military. Anti-American rallies actually occur in urban centers that have had little experience with drone strikes. Moreover, the media exaggerate the number of civilians killed, when drone strikes have in fact become quite precise. Although the United States must find a political way to put an end to militant fundamentalism, drone strikes have caused psychological fear among militants and restricted their operations, thus tilting the balance of power towards US interests.

Regardless of what the news agencies in Pakistan claim about the negative effects of drone strikes, the weapon is proving to be a game changer for the U.S. war on terrorism. And surprisingly, the Pakistani Army quietly admits to this fact. Just the way Stinger missiles shifted the balance of power in favor of the United States in the 1980s, drones are producing the same results.

The critics of unmanned strikes, who claim that drones are contributing to growing radicalization in Pakistan, haven't looked around enough—or they would realize that much of the radicalization already was established by the Taliban in the 1990s. The real tragedy is that it is acceptable for the Taliban to radicalize and kill, but it is considered a breach of sovereignty for the United States, in pursuit of those radicalizing Pakistan's people, to do the same.

There is so much protest over the drones because the media reports about them are biased. Although people on ground in war zones contend that the drone strikes have very few civilian casualties and, with time, have become extremely precise, the media presents quite a different story to boost its ratings.

There isn't as much anti-Americanism as one would suspect in areas where the United States is conducting drone strikes.

Many in Pakistan, especially in the army, understand the positive impact of this weapon. Drones are coming in handy for two reasons: their precision and psychological effect. Many analysts of this subject have been concerned only with the military aspect, such as whether or not drones are precise enough and the casualties they incur. But part of what works in favor of the United States is the psychological impact—the fear that drones have instilled in the militants. The fact that the United States might strike day or night, inside the militant compound or outside while traveling in the convoys, works to deter militants and restrict their operations. This tilts the balance of power in favor of the United States.

Most of the people in the Pakistani Army whom I interviewed on the subject were positive about the drone strikes and their direct correlation with a decrease in terrorist attacks in Pakistan. The majority focused on the psychological impact of the drones and how they have put militants on the run, forcing them to sleep under trees at night, though it must be said that army officials showed some concern about cases in which the same psychological impact is experienced by civilians.

Locals I talked to are frustrated over the fear that they might get hit by a drone if the militants are hiding in their neighborhood. But this frustration may have a positive impact as it motivates civilians to flush out and close doors to militants who seek refuge in their areas.

Surprisingly, there isn't as much anti-Americanism as one would suspect in areas where the United States is conducting drone strikes, largely because the locals are fed up with the influx of militants in their areas and have suffered because of terrorism. However, urban centers, which have suffered the least from terrorism, are far more radicalized and anti-American. Hence, we see large anti-drone rallies in the cities of Punjab, where people have little first-hand experience with drones. The anti-American lot in these places will start a rally for any reason at all as long as they get to burn a few American flags.

Pakistan's army remains worried about the domestic political repercussions of drone strikes. The army has been weakened already by its rift with the civilian government, and increasing pressure from the United States likely will continue that trend. With a low approval rating, the army is nervous about dealing with the growing sentiment against drone strikes, no matter how effective they have been recently. The Pakistan People's Party also is worried, having taken blows from the judiciary and the opposition. Recent media reports claiming a secret, backdoor deal between the Pakistan People's

Party government and the United States over the drone strikes have further delegitimized the party.

These concerns about the civilian impact of drones are genuine, and the United States will have to address them. Drone operators must become more precise and accurate in their targeting and intelligence gathering. This can be done only through unconditional cooperation with Pakistan, which requires being sensitive to that country's domestic political conditions.

Pakistan and the United States also need to be careful about drone strikes possibly pushing militants deeper into Pakistani cities. Drones will be useless if security forces are unable to stop a migration of militants into urban centers. Likewise, the United States will have serious challenges gaining permission for drone strikes outside tribal areas without improvements in diplomatic relations.

While drones are successful today, the United States must remember that it will be only a matter of time before militants find a way to hide from unmanned attacks. As such, drone operations ultimately must be accompanied by a political solution. The United States finds itself in a stronger bargaining position due to the use of drones, and it must make good use of this opportunity.

5

The Ease of Drone Warfare Raises Serious Moral Questions

John Kaag and Sarah Kreps

John Kaag is an assistant professor of philosophy at the University of Massachusetts at Lowell. Sarah Kreps is an assistant professor of government at Cornell University.

Unlike other forms of modern technology that make life easier, drones raise serious moral questions. When something is easy, it can become habit. However, in war, decision makers should think long and hard before using advanced weapons. In addition, while the threat of mutually assured destruction provided a safeguard against the use of nuclear weapons, the use of drones against an enemy without this technology creates an imbalance of power that increases the risk of oppression. Moreover, although the accuracy of drones appears to distinguish between combatants and civilians, the combatant status of current drone targets is unclear. Thus, clear ethical and legal guidelines should regulate drone use.

Killing with drones is a turning point in the ethical complexity of war.

The moral case for military drones is not like the moral case for modern medicine, where there is a broad consensus that its use results in a clear increase in human welfare. At the risk of understatement, the case for combat-ready unmanned

John Kaag and Sarah Kreps, "Opinion: Drones End War's Easy Morality," *The Chronicle of Higher Education*, vol. 59, no. 3, September 14, 2012. Reproduced by permission.

aerial vehicles is more vexed. Similarly, the case against combat drones is not like the argument against nuclear holocaust or firebombing (like in Dresden or Tokyo[1]). When it comes to warfare, the age of seemingly easy moral decision making is over.

Perhaps this comes as a disappointment.

Amid our iPads, microwaves, and industrialized agriculture, it is tempting to think that everything, including the task of acting morally in war, should come easily. This is the temptation of our technological age. In response, we offer an unpopular argument: When it comes to war, if it's easy, it's probably not moral.

Reasons for Moral Pause

More carefully put, the ease of a particular action (such as the killing of 15 people in North Waziristan [Pakistan] in June [2012] by a U.S. drone strike) should give us moral pause for at least three reasons. First, easy actions are often carried out habitually, without the reflection that's required for moral responsibility. Complacency is not the stuff of moral decisions. Second, easy actions often reflect an imbalance in power (think of how easy it is to exploit oppressed individuals, who are unable to resist their oppression), and these same actions are often unjust (think of the injustice involved in this oppression). The institutions of oppression, those that create problematic power differentials, are self-perpetuating and opaque. Third, as philosophers since Plato have observed, actions undertaken in the name of self-interest are often the easiest to accomplish. Self-interest, however, should not be confused with moral justification—even if it is easy to do so.

---

1. The authors refer to the dropping of high-explosive and incendiary devices on these two cities near the end of World War II. The attack on Dresden, Germany, led to the destruction of fifteen square miles of the city and the death of as many as 25,000 people. Multiple air raids on Tokyo, Japan, destroyed as much as half of the city and led to the death of as many as 100,000 people. People continue to debate whether these attacks were necessary or were in fact immoral.

"We must catch up morally and internationally with the machine age. We must catch up with it, and we must catch up with it in such a way as to create peace in the world, or it will destroy us and everybody else." When President Harry S. Truman spoke those words on April 17, 1947, he did so at a unique moment in military history. America was in the early phases of developing thermonuclear weapons, culminating in the testing of the first hydrogen bomb in 1952. The Soviets followed suit, and in 1961 tested what became known as the "Tsar Bomb," the most powerful nuclear device ever detonated, estimated at 3,800 times the force of the bomb dropped on Hiroshima.

Truman called for a new type of moral decision making that would guard against nuclear holocaust. As it turned out, thermonuclear conflagration served as its own safeguard. Mutual assured destruction [MAD], the informal policy that was accepted to a greater or lesser extent all the way through the cold war, didn't rest on a moral rationale but on the principle of self-preservation, a principle with questionable moral status. Think of two barroom fighters who, after sizing each other up, decide that it's best to call it a day. That judgment would be prudent but not moral in any meaningful sense of the word. The logic of MAD was simple: We would not bomb someone who could bomb us back. Cost-benefit analysis stood in rather nicely for moral deliberation.

Our reliance on precision weaponry has become a stand-in for making hard moral or legal distinctions.

Catching Up Morally

For better or worse, that time is over. We have entered the drone age.

Never have the array of strategic choices been so expansive for modern militaries; never have modern militaries faced the question of ethics in such a pointed way. In the words of Franklin D. Roosevelt, "great power involves great responsibility." We can now see that this is not some finger-wagging moralism. Roosevelt is stating an ethical truism: Only those who have power, who have freedom of choice, can be deemed truly good or blameworthy. Drones and precision-guided weapons give the United States unprecedented control over the battlefield. And therefore, Truman's plea to "catch up morally" has begun to make sense. The question of waging a truly just war—one that has preoccupied philosophers for nearly a thousand years—can finally be asked in a meaningful way.

Interestingly and disturbingly, the technologies that allow us to uphold just-war principles also obscure the moral and legal complexities of modern warfare. The surveillance capabilities of drones and the accuracy of precision-guided weapons are purported to allow militaries to uphold the just-war tenet of "distinction," which insists on the separate treatments of combatants and noncombatants. Indeed, the mere use of these technologies is often seen as proof that the distinction has been observed. In truth, however, targeting has become ever trickier. This difficulty is masked by catch-all expressions like "terrorist," "suspected militant," "contingency threats," or "covered person"—all of which have been used to describe legitimate targets in U.S. drone strikes. But none of these vague terms prove the legitimacy of targets. What exactly is a covered person?

The rhetoric and moral thinking about war has become woollier as our weaponry has become more precise. And our reliance on precision weaponry has become a stand-in for making hard moral or legal distinctions. But our trust in technology is dangerously misplaced. Combatant status cannot be determined by an algorithm. Instead, we should recognize the unshakeably human character of war, and identify new ethical and legal resources to regulate armed conflict.

The concept of just war has been around for centuries, but up until this point, warfare resembled nasty brawls or barroom standoffs that rarely afforded aggressors the time to reflect on the concept of justice without endangering their troops or themselves. The moment of calm reflection—that moment that defines the business of ethics—is upon us. Thanks to the technological advantage of precision-guided munitions and drones, we are now responsible if we squander it.

6

Drones Should Not Be Used as an International Law-Enforcement Tool

Mary Ellen O'Connell

Mary Ellen O'Connell is a law professor at the University of Notre Dame and a research professor of international dispute resolution at the Kroc Institute, a center that studies the causes of violent conflict and strategies for sustainable peace.

Although the United States may use drones in armed conflict, using drones to kill terrorists outside of the justice system violates international law. Law enforcement officials must warn before they use their weapons and may only do so in self-defense or when facing imminent death. CIA drone strikes, however, do not meet these requirements. Moreover, terrorists are criminals, and labeling them enemy combatants in order to justify drone strikes elevates their status. Drone strikes also kill innocent civilians. While the law of armed conflict recognizes that some civilians may die to meet a military goal, law enforcement must protect civilians from harm. Since drone strikes appear to fuel rather than reduce terrorism, the United States should limit their use to the battlefield.

Combat drones are battlefield weapons. They fire missiles or drop bombs capable of inflicting very serious damage. Drones are not lawful for use outside combat zones. Outside

Mary Ellen O'Connell, "Lawful Use of Combat Drones," Statement for the House Subcommittee on National Security & Foreign Affairs, Hearing: Rise of the Drones II: Examining the Legality of Unmanned Targeting, April 28, 2010.

such zones, police are the proper law enforcement agents and police are generally required to warn before using lethal force. Restricting drones to the battlefield is the most important single rule governing their use. Yet, the United States is failing to follow it more often than not. At the very time we are trying to win hearts and minds to respect the rule of law, we are ourselves failing to respect a very basic rule: remote weapons systems belong on the battlefield.

A Lawful Battlefield Weapon

The United States first used weaponized drones during the combat in Afghanistan that began on October 7, 2001. We requested permission from Uzbekistan, which was then hosting the U.S. airbase where drones were kept. We also used combat drones in the battles with Iraq's armed forces in the effort to topple Saddam Hussein's government that began in March 2003. We are still using drones lawfully in the on-going combat in Afghanistan. Drones spare the lives of pilots, since the unmanned aerial vehicle is flown from a site far from the attack zone. If a drone is shot down, there is no loss of human life. Moreover, on the battlefield drones can be more protective of civilian lives than high aerial bombing or long-range artillery. Their cameras can pick up details about the presence of civilians. Drones can fly low and target more precisely using this information. General McChrystal has wisely insisted on zero-tolerance for civilian deaths in Afghanistan. The use of drones can help us achieve that.

What drones cannot do is comply with police rules for the use of lethal force away from the battlefield. In law enforcement it must be possible to warn before using lethal force, in war-fighting this is not necessary, making the use of bombs and missiles lawful.

The United Nations Basic Principles for the Use of Force and Firearms by Law Enforcement Officials (*UN Basic Principles*) set out the international legal standard for the use of force by police:

Law enforcement officials shall not use firearms against persons except in self-defense or defense of others against the imminent threat of death or serious injury, to prevent the perpetration of a particularly serious crime involving grave threat to life, to arrest a person presenting such a danger and resisting their authority, or to prevent his or her escape, and only when less extreme means are insufficient to achieve these objectives. In any event, intentional lethal use of firearms may only be made when strictly unavoidable in order to protect life.

The United States has failed to follow these rules by using combat drones in places where no actual armed conflict was occurring or where the U.S. was not involved in the armed conflict.

For much of the period that the United States has used drones on the territory of Pakistan, there has been no armed conflict.

The Improper Use of Drones

On November 3, 2002, the CIA used a drone to fire laser-guided Hellfire missiles at a passenger vehicle traveling in a thinly populated region of Yemen. At that time, the Air Force controlled the entire drone fleet, but the Air Force rightly raised concerns about the legality of attacking in a place where there was no armed conflict. CIA agents based in Djibouti carried out the killing. All six passengers in the vehicle were killed, including an American. In January 2003, the United Nations Commission on Human Rights received a report on the Yemen strike from its special rapporteur[1] on extrajudicial, summary, or arbitrary killing. The rapporteur concluded that the strike constituted "a clear case of extrajudicial killing."

1. Rapporteur is a French-derived word for an investigator who reports to a deliberative body. United Nations special rapporteurs are people who receive a specific mandate from a body such as the United Nations Human Rights Council to investigate possible human rights abuses.

Apparently, Yemen gave tacit consent for the strike. States cannot, however, give consent to a right they do not have. States may not use military force against individuals on their territory when law enforcement measures are appropriate. At the time of the strike, Yemen was not using military force anywhere on its territory. More recently, Yemen has been using military force to suppress militants in two parts of the country. The U.S.'s on-going drone use, however, has not been part of those campaigns.

The United States has also used combat drones in Somalia probably starting in late 2006 during the Ethiopian invasion when the U.S. assisted Ethiopia in its attempt to install a new government in that volatile country. Ethiopia's effort had some support from the UN and the African Union. To the extent that the U.S. was assisting Ethiopia, our actions had some justification. It is clear, however, that the U.S. has used drone strikes independently of the attempt to restore order in Somalia. The U.S. has continued to target and kill individuals in Somalia following Ethiopia's pullout from the country.

The U.S. use of drones in Pakistan has similar problems to the uses in Yemen and Somalia. Where military force *is* warranted to address internal violence, governments have widely resorted to the practice of inviting in another state to assist. This is the legal justification the U.S. cites for its use of military force today in Afghanistan and Iraq. Yet, the U.S. cannot point to invitations from Pakistan for most of its drone attacks. Indeed, for much of the period that the United States has used drones on the territory of Pakistan, there has been no armed conflict. Therefore, even express consent by Pakistan would not justify their use.

The United States has been carrying out drone attacks in Pakistan since 2004. Pakistani authorities only began to use major military force to suppress militancy in May 2009, in Buner Province. Some U.S. drone strikes have been coordinated with Islamabad's efforts, but some have not. Some strikes have apparently even targeted groups allied with Islamabad.

The Battlefield Defined

The Bush administration justified the 2002 Yemen strike and others as justified under the law of armed conflict in the "Global War on Terror." The current State Department Legal Adviser, Harold Koh, has rejected the term "Global War on Terror," preferring to base our actions on the view that the U.S. is in an "armed conflict with al-Qaeda, the Taliban and associated forces." Under the new label, the U.S. is carrying out many of the same actions as the Bush administration under the old one: using lethal force without warning, far from any actual battlefield.

Armed conflict, however, is a real thing. The United States is currently engaged in an armed conflict in Afghanistan. The United States has tens of thousands of highly trained troops fighting battles with a well-organized opponent that is able to hold territory. The situation in Afghanistan today conforms to the definition of armed conflict in international law. The International Law Association's Committee on the Use of Force issued a report in 2008 confirming the basic characteristics of all armed conflict: 1.) the presence of organized armed groups that are 2.) engaged in intense inter-group fighting. The fighting or hostilities of an armed conflict occurs within limited zones, referred to as combat or conflict zones. It is only in such zones that killing enemy combatants or those taking a direct part in hostilities is permissible.

Because armed conflict requires a certain intensity of fighting, the isolated terrorist attack, regardless of how serious the consequences, is not an armed conflict. Terrorism is crime. Members of al Qaeda or other terrorist groups are active in Canada, France, Germany, Indonesia, Morocco, Saudi Arabia, Spain, the United Kingdom, Yemen and elsewhere. Still, these countries do not consider themselves in a war with al Qaeda. In the words of a leading expert on the law of armed conflict, the British Judge on the International Court of Justice, Sir Christopher Greenwood:

> In the language of international law there is no basis for speaking of a war on Al-Qaeda or any other terrorist group, for such a group cannot be a belligerent, it is merely a band of criminals, and to treat it as anything else risks distorting the law while giving that group a status which to some implies a degree of legitimacy.

Elevating Terrorist Status

To label terrorists "enemy combatants" lifts them out of the status of *criminal* to that of *combatant*, the same category as America's own troops on the battlefield. This move to label terrorists combatants is contrary to strong historic trends. From earliest times, governments have struggled to prevent their enemies from approaching a status of equality. Even governments on the verge of collapse due to the pressure of a rebel advance have vehemently denied that the violence inflicted by their enemies was anything but criminal violence. Governments fear the psychological and legal advantages to opponents of calling them "combatants" and their struggle a "war."

The U.S.'s actions . . . are generally consistent with its long-term policy of separating acts of terrorism from armed conflict—except when it comes to drones.

President Ronald Reagan strongly opposed labeling terrorists combatants. He said that to "grant combatant status to irregular forces even if they do not satisfy the traditional requirements . . . would endanger civilians among whom terrorists and other irregulars attempt to conceal themselves."

The United Kingdom and other allies take the same position as President Reagan: "It is the understanding of the United Kingdom that the term 'armed conflict' of itself and in its context denotes a situation of a kind which is not constituted by the commission of ordinary crimes including acts of terrorism whether concerted or in isolation."

In the United States and other countries plagued by al Qaeda, institutions are functioning normally. No one has declared martial law. The International Committee of the Red Cross is not active. Criminal trials of suspected terrorists are being held in regular criminal courts. The police use lethal force only in situations of necessity. The U.S.'s actions today are generally consistent with its long-term policy of separating acts of terrorism from armed conflict—except when it comes to drones.

Only members of the United States armed forces have the combatant's privilege to use lethal force without facing prosecution.

Battlefield Restraints

Even when the U.S. is using drones at the request of Pakistan in battles it is waging, we are failing to follow important battlefield rules. The U.S. must respect the principles of necessity, proportionality and humanity in carrying out drone attacks. "Necessity" refers to military necessity, and the obligation that force is used only if necessary to accomplish a reasonable military objective. "Proportionality" prohibits that "which may be expected to cause incidental loss of civilian life, injury to civilians, damage to civilian objects, or a combination thereof, which would be excessive in relation to concrete and direct military advantage anticipated." These limitations on permissible force extend to both the quantity of force used and the geographic scope of its use.

Far from suppressing militancy in Pakistan, drone attacks are fueling the interest in fighting against the United States. This impact makes the use of drones difficult to justify under the terms of military necessity. Most serious of all, perhaps, is the disproportionate impact of drone attacks. A principle that provides context for all decisions in armed conflict is the principle of humanity. The principle of humanity supports decisions in favor of sparing life and avoiding destruction in close cases under either the principles of necessity or proportionality. According [to] the International Committee of the Red Cross, the principles of necessity and humanity are particularly important in situations such as Pakistan:

> In classic large-scale confrontations between well-equipped and organized armed forces or groups, the principles of military necessity and of humanity are unlikely to restrict the use of force against legitimate military targets beyond what is already required by specific provisions of IHL. The practical importance of their restraining function will increase with the ability of a party to the conflict to control the circumstances and area in which its military operations are conducted, and may become decisive where armed forces operate against selected individuals in situations comparable to peacetime policing. In practice, such considerations are likely to become particularly relevant where a party to the conflict exercises effective territorial control, most notably in occupied territories and non-international armed conflicts.

Another issue in drone use is the fact that strikes are carried out in Pakistan by the CIA and civilian contractors. Only members of the United States armed forces have the combatant's privilege to use lethal force without facing prosecution. CIA operatives are not trained in the law of armed conflict. They are not bound by the Uniform Code of Military Justice to respect the laws and customs of war. They are not subject to the military chain of command. This fact became abundantly clear during the revelation of U.S. use of harsh interrogation tactics. Given the negative impact of that unlawful conduct on America's standing in the world and our ability to promote the rule of law, it is difficult to fathom why the Obama administration is using the CIA to carry out drone attacks, let alone civilian contractors.

The use of military force in counter-terrorism operations has been counter-productive. Military force is a blunt instrument. Inevitably unintended victims are the result of almost any military action. Drone attacks in Pakistan have resulted in large numbers of deaths and are generally seen as fueling terrorism, not abating it. In Congressional testimony in March 2009, counter-terrorism expert, David Kilcullen, said drones in Pakistan are giving "rise to a feeling of anger that coalesces the population around the extremists and leads to spikes of extremism well outside the parts of the country where we are mounting those attacks." Another expert told the *New York Times*, "The more the drone campaign works, the more it fails—as increased attacks only make the Pakistanis angrier at the collateral damage and sustained violation of their sovereignty." A National Public Radio Report on April 26, 2010, pointed out that al Qaeda is losing support in the Muslim world because of its violent, lawless tactics. We can help eliminate the last of that support by distinguishing ourselves through commitment to the rule of law, especially by strict compliance with the rules governing lethal force.

7

CIA Drone Pilots Are Not Violating International Laws of War

Charles G. Kels

Charles G. Kels is a major in the Air Force Reserve and an attorney for the US Department of Homeland Security.

Claims that drone pilots violate international law when targeting terrorists are flawed. Nations have the right to self defense. Thus, when terrorists attacked the United States, the nation's leaders declared war on terrorists who would attack America. CIA drone pilots are not murderers but acting on behalf of the United States in this war. Claims that CIA drone pilots do not wear the uniform of soldiers fail to recognize that the purpose of military uniforms is to distinguish soldiers from civilians, which is irrelevant in the case of drone pilots. In the end, whether to use CIA agents or soldiers as drone pilots is a question of policy not international law.

One of the more pernicious accusations made by opponents of U.S. targeted killing operations is that CIA personnel involved in drone warfare are violating the law. This argument, endorsed by many in the legal academy and human rights community, is meant to delegitimize the CIA counterterrorism offensive by equating its operators with the transnational terrorists they are targeting.

Charles G. Kels, "Why There's Nothing Illegal About CIA Drone Pilots," *Small Wars Journal*, August 3, 2012. Copyright © 2012 by Small Wars Journal. All rights reserved. Reproduced by permission.

However, such criminations are based on an overly rigid and inaccurate reading of the laws of war.

Countering the Drone-Strike Critics

As a preliminary matter, the stated U.S. position is that the fight against al Qaeda constitutes an armed conflict sanctioned domestically by the post-9/11 Authorization for the Use of Military Force, and internationally by the inherent right of self-defense acknowledged in the United Nations Charter.

The law of armed conflict, which governs the conduct of hostilities during wartime, does not prohibit the use of civilian personnel in combat. Rather, Additional Protocol I to the Geneva Conventions outlaws "perfidy," or the deliberate manipulation of the rules of war to put law-abiding fighters at risk. Such conduct, which our enemies engage in constantly, includes "the feigning of civilian, non-combatant status" in order to mount ambushes.

The legal requirement for fighters to display a distinguishing marker emphatically does not mean that even military service members must be in uniform 24 hours a day.

Although Protocol I applies only under specified circumstances and the U.S. has not ratified it, we nonetheless acknowledge the prohibition on perfidy as binding customary law. Thus, it would be unlawful for the CIA to paint a drone with the insignia of a commercial airline carrier, and then use such camouflage to launch sneak attacks on civilian airports.

Since the use of CIA drone operators is not illegal per se, the next issue is the status of its workforce under the law of armed conflict. This discussion is largely academic, because it considers whether CIA pilots would merit status as prisoners of war (POWs) if captured. Of course, no one imagines that al Qaeda would apply a legal analysis to this question, which at least partly explains why the physical remove of drone technology is so valuable in a fight against lawless enemies.

As a general rule, soldiers in war are entitled to "belligerent immunity," which means that because they are authorized to directly participate in hostilities, they cannot be held liable for the warlike acts they commit. As the famed Nuremberg prosecutor Telford Taylor wrote, "War consists largely of acts that would be criminal if performed in time of peace," but "the state of war lays a blanket of immunity over its warriors." As such, enemy soldiers captured on the battlefield are held as POWs rather than tried as murderers.

The third Geneva Convention lays out a four-part test that armed groups must meet in order to qualify for POW status. Although these criteria are technically applicable in limited scenarios, they have gained larger acceptance over time as the indicia of lawful belligerency in general. The threshold factors include: (1) command responsibility, (2) distinctive insignia, (3) exposed weaponry, and (4) compliance with the laws of war.

Questioning the Uniform Requirement

Critics of U.S. targeting operations often contend that because CIA drone pilots are not sitting at their consoles in flight suits bearing Air Force rank insignia, they are entitled to neither belligerent immunity nor POW status, and could be tried for murder under the domestic laws of any foreign authority that apprehended them. While there are no doubt certain countries that would relish just such an opportunity, this is not a legally defensible assertion.

First, the legal requirement for fighters to display a distinguishing marker emphatically does not mean that even military service members must be in uniform 24 hours a day. In fact, because soldiers are valid military targets at all times during war, it is anticipated that if attacked while sleeping, they will immediately fight back in their underwear rather than wait to don their battle dress. Moreover, many an epic sea battle has been fought by sailors in shirtsleeves.

Second, it is important not to lose sight of the underlying principle animating the formalized requirements. Here, the basic rule is "distinction," which requires belligerents to distinguish themselves from nearby civilians so as not to bring them into the enemy's line of fire. This standard, although routinely and purposefully violated by our adversaries' use of human shields, has no bearing on the attire of a drone operator at Langley.

While there is certainly room for debate over the proper role of intelligence agents in lethal operations, this is a matter of policy, not law. Branding CIA operators as scofflaws simply for doing their jobs is neither productive nor correct.

8

New International Laws to Govern the Use of Drones Are Needed

America Magazine

America Magazine *is a weekly Catholic magazine.*

Policy makers design international laws of armed conflict to hold those who use lethal force accountable. These laws, however, do not address concerns about the use of drones to target terrorists in other nations. Although terrorists pose a threat to the United States, their execution by drone strike without due process is troublesome for a democratic nation. Moreover, current international laws prohibit military strikes in nations not at war. Indeed, US drone strikes erode interpretations of international law that may lead to the abuse of drones by others. Thus, the United States and nations worldwide need new international laws to address these concerns.

Drone warfare presents new challenges to the way the United States wages war. Under President Obama drone attacks have become the characteristic way this country fights terrorism. The United States now routinely employs drone attacks in Afghanistan, Pakistan, Somalia and Yemen. Recent revelations by the reporters David E. Sanger (in *The New York Times* and *Confront and Conceal*) and Daniel Klaidman (*Kill or Capture*) make it possible now to do informed ethical and legal analyses of the president's use of drones in counter-terrorist attacks on Al Qaeda and its confederates.

The Problem with Targeted Strikes

Drone strikes are now conducted out of the White House, with the president himself approving targets. The president's direct role in this process is problematic. The head of a democratic state should have distance from the application of force, both to avoid the risk of international prosecution for wrongful use of force and also to ensure that those professionally responsible for the control of force are accountable to a system of military justice and international humanitarian law. To that end, the Law of Armed Conflict needs to be updated to include issues of counter-terrorist drone warfare, and intelligence services routinely engaged in antiterrorist attacks should be made subject to it.

Another practice requiring closer attention is that of signature strikes, so-called because facts on the ground, particularly the presence of fighting-age men, are taken as a "signature" of terrorist activity and therefore of a legitimate target. Without further on-the-ground intelligence, however, it is hard to know whether such clusters are made up of convinced terrorists or mere bystanders. So the conventions of military ethics that make those who actively threaten the United States legitimate objects of direct attack are stretched in a way that will inevitably result in the deaths of nonthreatening civilians. Clearer restraints on signature attacks are necessary.

The proliferation of drone technologies . . . [points] to the urgent need for an international convention to set standards for the use of drones in cross-border operations.

The targeting of alleged terrorists also raises questions of extrajudicial killing of suspects without due process. The experience of the selling of the Iraq War in 2003 by means of false and mistaken information should make the public dubious of intelligence as a warrant for execution from the air. Due process must mean more than careful deliberation by officials. The authority and conditions for killing suspected terrorists must be clarified in both U.S. and international law. U.S. antiterrorist law ought to reflect John Adams's proposition that ours must be a government of laws, not of men.

The Principles of Sovereignty and Noninterference

The ability of drones to penetrate foreign air space has also played havoc with traditional principles of sovereignty and noninterference along with the prohibition in international humanitarian law against military strikes on neutral territory. In the past, these principles deterred attacks on foreign soil. The spread of global terrorism and the availability of smart weaponry, however, have eroded those diplomatic restraints; and President Obama has invoked the right to self-defense in ordering these attacks even when the local governments object.

Sovereignty and noninterference play important roles in reducing the occasions for armed conflict. No one exception harms the rules, but the cumulative effect of repeated violations is deleterious for the international system. As President Obama insists, the United States does have a duty to protect its citizens from attack, arguably even to striking on foreign soil when a second government cannot or will not police the terrorists on its own. But the more the United States invokes the self-defense justification in attacks on foreign soil, the more other countries have an incentive to do the same.

Already world public opinion has come to resent the freedom with which the United States employs drone strikes in its antiterrorist campaign. At the same time, more than 50 countries now possess drones. (In late June [2012] Bolivian police destroyed 240 jungle drug labs detected by Brazilian surveillance drones.) How long will it be before one or more nations begin to employ these weapons for cross-border strikes? How long will it be before terrorists target drones against sites within the United States? The proliferation of drone technologies and the growing risk of their use by rogue regimes and terrorist groups point to the urgent need for an international convention to set standards for the use of drones in cross-border operations.

Absent an international convention, U.S. interest lies in upholding international standards for nonintervention even as diplomats work in the long term to adapt international law to the reality of combat with non-state actors, like Al Qaeda. Given the proliferation of drone technology, American exceptionalism in its application will be short-lived. The United States can better advance its long-term security with a global compact than without one.

9

How Drones Are Used to Fight Terrorism Requires Public Debate

Ben Iannotta

Ben Iannotta is editor of C4ISR Journal, *a monthly publication covering emerging issues and trends in global military warfare technologies.*

Although drone strikes are clearly necessary, their use to kill enemies in foreign countries requires public debate. Americans need assurance that the nation's national security strategy is effective and does not instead create more terrorists. While the details of drone strikes must remain secret to be successful, the public should know the scope of drone use. Moreover, lawmakers must assure the public through persistent oversight that decision makers only use drones when based on the best intelligence. Americans need to know that the United States does not use drones merely because it can but because they are the best tool to fight terrorism.

It's messy to watch, but the interplay of news coverage, politics and congressional oversight is playing out just as it should in the matter of the CIA's drone strikes.

Debating the Role of Drone Strikes

The Obama administration's sudden transparency about the drone war—Republicans chalk it up to the president wanting to look tough in an election year—has sparked a long-overdue

Ben Iannotta, "Editorial: Debate the Drone War," *Defense News,* June 28, 2012. Reproduced by permission.

public debate about the appropriate role and scope of the administration's policy of robotically killing enemies in distant lands. This debate is not necessarily what the administration intended, but the unpredictability of the public forum is one of the key strengths of modern government.

When columnist Charles Krauthammer pointed out that you can't interrogate a dead man, and that routinely vaporizing terror suspects "yields no intelligence about terror networks or terror plans," he gave national voice to an opinion expressed quietly by dissenters in the intelligence community. He struck a chord with the public on that point and with his charges of a White House double standard: "festooning" prisoners with rights while summarily killing suspects. The *Washington Post* reported receiving 2,700 comments on Krauthammer's June 4 [2012] column.

Whether the issue is secret prisons, extraordinary renditions or drone strikes, national security policy is strengthened, not weakened, when the public is included in the conversation.

Few experts, including Krauthammer, think the drone strikes should be halted or that the U.S. should return to its pre-Sept. 11 complacency. In those days, neither the Clinton nor Bush administrations showed sufficient zeal for targeting Osama bin Laden, despite rock-solid CIA intelligence that he was targeting us. But in today's context, congressional overseers should explore whether the pendulum has swung too far in the other direction.

Understanding the Impact of Drones

Lawmakers should demand to know how a high-volume drone-strike campaign in Yemen and the tribal areas of Pakistan fits into America's larger national security strategy. Does the take-no-prisoners policy—to borrow Krauthammer's term—make it easier for al-Qaida to recruit terrorists? Does it undercut the goal of forging a more positive relationship with Muslim cultures? Does it sacrifice broader intelligence opportunities?

So far, the House and Senate intelligence committees appear to be more concerned about plugging leaks than finding answers to those questions. It is true that the White House needs to stop leaks that could compromise specific operations, but the intelligence committees should not fear public dialogue about the appropriateness of the policies that drive those operations. Whether the issue is secret prisons, extraordinary renditions or drone strikes, national security policy is strengthened, not weakened, when the public is included in the conversation. A realist would recognize the impossibility of entirely shrouding endeavors like those in our open society, and the loss of the moral high ground when they are revealed.

As for the merits of the drone strikes, dogged oversight by the intelligence committees will be crucial. The U.S. public has every right to know about the broad scale and scope of the drone campaign, but relies on hard-charging lawmakers with clearances to oversee the evidence justifying individual strikes. The public can't be privy to that evidence before a killing, because that would compromise the ability to carry out an operation if a strike were in fact justified. In short, without poring over the evidence the president sees, it's hard for anyone on the outside to conclude authoritatively that there are too many strikes.

The sheer volume, however, suggests that a low threshold is in place for applying deadly force. Lawmakers must look closely at that threshold in the context of the country's overall strategic goals to make sure the strikes are helping, not harming, national security in the long run.

The drone war must not become a case of politicians employing weapons simply because they can.

10

The Domestic Use of Drones Poses Serious Threats to Civil Liberties

John W. Whitehead

John W. Whitehead is an attorney and author who has written and practiced widely in the area of constitutional law and human rights. In 1982, he established The Rutherford Institute, a nonprofit civil liberties and human rights organization.

As is often the case with military technology, the drone was quickly recognized by law enforcement officials for its potential uses within US borders. In fact, while drone technology may appear new, US border security agencies have used drones to patrol America's borders for years. Unfortunately, surveillance drones do not discriminate between lawbreakers and law-abiding citizens. Moreover, since the goal of law enforcement is to anticipate and prevent crime, under the pretext of keeping people safe, drones will eventually be used to control and contain people. To do so, law enforcement officials will likely weaponize domestic drones. Therefore, before their use becomes standard, Americans should work to limit the domestic use of drones.

> "A standing military force, with an overgrown Executive will not long be safe companions to liberty. The means of defence against foreign danger, have been always the instruments of tyranny at home."—James Madison

John W. Whitehead, "Commentary: Drones over America: Tyranny at Home," The Rutherford Institute website, June 28, 2010. www.rutherford.org. Copyright © 2010 by The Rutherford Institute. All rights reserved. Reproduced by permission.

The U.S. government has a history of commandeering military technology for use against Americans. We saw this happen with tear gas, tasers and sound cannons, all of which were first used on the battlefield before being deployed against civilians at home. Now the drones—pilotless, remote controlled aircraft that have been used in Iraq and Afghanistan—are coming home to roost.

The Potential for Broad Domestic Drone Use

Drones, a $2 billion cornerstone of the Obama administration's war efforts, have increasingly found favor with both military and law enforcement officials. "The more we have used them," stated Defense Secretary Robert Gates, "the more we have identified their potential in a broader and broader set of circumstances."

Now the Federal Aviation Administration (FAA) is facing mounting pressure from state governments and localities to issue flying rights for a range of unmanned aerial vehicles (UAVs) to carry out civilian and law-enforcement activities. As the Associated Press reports, "Tornado researchers want to send them into storms to gather data. Energy companies want to use them to monitor pipelines. State police hope to send them up to capture images of speeding cars' license plates. Local police envision using them to track fleeing suspects." Unfortunately, to a drone, everyone is a suspect because drone technology makes no distinction between the law-abiding individual and the suspect. Everyone gets monitored, photographed, tracked and targeted.

The FAA, citing concerns over the need to regulate air traffic and establish anti-collision rules for the aircrafts and their operators, has thus far been reluctant to grant broad approval for the use of UAVs in American airspace. However, unbeknownst to most Americans, remote controlled aircraft have been employed domestically for years now. They were first used as a national security tool for patrolling America's borders and then as a means of monitoring citizens. For example, back in 2006, the Los Angeles County Sheriff's Department was testing out a SkySeer drone for use in police work. With a 6.5-foot wingspan, the lightweight SkySeer can be folded up like a kite and stored in a shoulder pack. At 250 feet, it can barely be seen with the naked eye.

Eventually ... police departments and intelligence agencies will make drones a routine part of their operations. However, you can be sure they won't limit themselves to just surveillance.

As another news story that same year reported, "one North Carolina county is using a UAV equipped with low-light and infrared cameras to keep watch on its citizens. The aircraft has been dispatched to monitor gatherings of motorcycle riders at the Gaston County fairgrounds from just a few hundred feet in the air—close enough to identify faces—and many more uses, such as the aerial detection of marijuana fields, are planned." In 2007, insect-like drones were seen hovering over political rallies in New York and Washington, seemingly spying on protesters. An eyewitness reported that the drones "looked kind of like dragonflies or little helicopters."

Dramatic Advances

Drone technology has advanced dramatically in the ensuing years, with surveillance drones getting smaller, more sophisticated and more lethal with each evolution. Modeling their prototype for a single-winged rotorcraft on the maple seed's unique design, aerospace engineering students at the University of Maryland have created the world's smallest controllable surveillance drones, capable of hovering to record conversations or movements of citizens.

Thus far, the domestic use of drones has been primarily for surveillance purposes and, as far as we know, has been limited in scope. Eventually, however, police departments and intelligence agencies will make drones a routine part of their operations. However, you can be sure they won't limit themselves to just surveillance.

Police today use whatever tools are at their disposal in order to anticipate and forestall crime. This means employing technology to attain total control. Technology, which functions without discrimination because it exists without discrimination, tends to be applied everywhere it can be applied. Thus, the logical aim of technologically equipped police who operate as technicians must be control, containment and eventually restriction of freedom.

The crucial question ... is whether Americans will be able to limit the government's use of [drone] surveillance tools or whether we will be caught in an electronic nightmare from which there is no escape.

Weaponizing Drones

In this way, under the guise of keeping Americans safe and controlled, airborne drones will have to be equipped with an assortment of lethal and nonlethal weapons in order to effectuate control of citizens on the ground. The arsenal of nonlethal weapons will likely include Long Range Acoustic Devices (LRADs), which are used to break up protests or riots by sending a piercing sound into crowds and can cause serious hearing damage; high-intensity strobe lights, which can cause dizziness, disorientation and loss of balance and make it virtually impossible to run away; and tasers, which administer a powerful electric shock.

Since June 2001, over 350 people, including women, children and elderly individuals, have died in the U.S. after being shocked with "non-lethal" tasers. "Imagine how incidents would skyrocket," notes Paul Joseph Watson for PrisonPlanet .com, "once the personal element of using a Taser is removed and they are strapped to marauding surveillance drones, eliminating any responsibility for deaths and injuries that occur."

"Also available to police," writes Watson, "will be a drone that can fire tear gas as well as rubber pellets to disperse anyone still living under the delusion that they were born in a democratic country." In fact, the French company Tecknisolar Seni has built a drone armed with a double-barreled 44 mm Flash-Ball gun. The one-kilo Flash-Ball resembles a large caliber handgun and fires so-called non-lethal rounds, including tear gas and rubber impact rounds to bring down a suspect. Despite being labeled a "non-lethal weapon," this, too, is not without its dangers. As David Hambling writes for *Wired News*, "Like other impact rounds, the Flash-Ball is meant to be aimed at the body—firing from a remote, flying platform is likely to increase the risk of head injury."

One thing is clear: while the idea of airborne drones policing America's streets may seem far-fetched, like something out of a sci-fi movie, it is no longer in the realm of the impossible. Now, it's just a matter of how soon you can expect them to be patrolling your own neighborhood. The crucial question, however, is whether Americans will be able to limit the government's use of such surveillance tools or whether we will be caught in an electronic nightmare from which there is no escape.

11

Drone, Sweet Drone

Micah Zenko

Micah Zenko is Douglas Dillon fellow with the Center for Preventive Action at the Council on Foreign Relations (a foreign policy think tank), who writes the CFR blog "Politics, Power, and Preventive Action."

Although Americans must be vigilant about how law-enforcement officials plan to use drones as a domestic law enforcement tool, many fears are unjustified. The media, for example, often perpetuate the inaccurate perception that all drones carry bombs or weapons, though Congress has prohibited the funding of armed drones for domestic use. Moreover, unlike the secrecy of the CIA's covert missions targeting terrorists, the public has access to information on the cost, location, and command and control structure of domestic drones. In truth, drones are a cost-effective solution to the US Customs and Border Protection's growing border-patrol demands and as such have significant public support.

*T*he debate over domestic drone surveillance is heating up. But don't panic yet.

Although the Department of Homeland Security's Customs and Border Protection (CBP) has been flying drones above U.S. borders for seven years, the drones' current uses, and potential expansion thereof, are now a contentious political issue. Last week, a Navy Global Hawk surveillance drone crashed just off the coast of Maryland. The very next day Sen. Rand Paul of Kentucky introduced the Preserving Freedom from Unwarranted Surveillance Act of 2012, which would limit the federal uses of drones within the United States to patrolling borders, preventing "imminent danger to life," and responding to high risk of a terrorist attack. The day after that, a prominent technology blog declared: "Revealed: 64 Drone Bases on American Soil."

Can we all take a deep breath?

Yes, such headlines feed the justified worries of many Americans about how drones could be used within the United States. Like other first-world security services, CBP fulfills its mandate largely by substituting remote monitoring and surveillance technology for human eyeballs on the ground. Of particular concern now is the prospect of a fleet of drones used by CBP that could potentially spy on—or, in some extreme versions, bomb—U.S. citizens. The conservative pundit Charles Krauthammer summarized one line of criticism in a recent rant about the prospect of domestic drones:

> I want a ban on this. Drones are instruments of war. The founders had a great aversion to any instruments of war, the use of the military, inside of the United States. They didn't like standing armies. It has all kinds of statutes against using the army in the country. A drone is a high-tech version of an old Army-issue musket. It ought to be used in Somalia to hunt the bad guys. But not in America.

Americans are right to be deeply concerned about the seemingly inevitable adoption of drones by federal, state, and local law enforcement, as well as by corporations and academic researchers. Currently, the Federal Aviation Administration (FAA) has provided approximately 300 certificates of authorization drones to fly over the United States, although some in the aerospace industry believe there could be as many as 30,000 in the skies by 2020. And the fears of many Americans are heightened by the lack of transparency and oversight of U.S. drone strikes abroad since the Sept. 11, 2001, attacks.

But much of the anxiety surrounding CBP drones—intensified by the false, yet oft-repeated, claim that the Environmental Protection Agency used "military-style drone planes to secretly observe livestock operations"—is overblown.

The House of Representatives stipulated: "None of the funds made available by this \[Department of Homeland Security funding\] Act may be used for the purchase, operation, or maintenance of armed unmanned aerial vehicles."

The CBP's reach is admittedly vast. It is the "largest law enforcement air force in the world," according to the Government Accountability Office (GAO), with an air fleet comprising more than 270 manned aircraft—including modern Blackhawk helicopters and P-3 Orion maritime surveillance planes—as well as a total of nine unarmed Predator B drones, which were deployed to the southwest border in 2005 and the northern border in 2009. Of greater concern are mobile Blackhawks, which are vastly more capable than their Predator cousins. According to a CBP official's recent congressional testimony, "The new and converted Black Hawks offer greater speed and endurance, greater lift capacity, more sophisticated onboard data processing . . . the ideal platform for confronting border violence and supporting operations in hostile environments." Now that's scary!

Yet despite its sizeable fleet of manned and unmanned aircraft, CBP is already unable to meet increasing border patrol demands—which include detecting illegal activity, conducting search-and-rescue missions, surveying natural disaster areas or Mississippi River levees, and transporting agents and equipment—on top of its day-to-day responsibilities, such as fostering trade and travel flows into the United States. The agency is responsible for guarding and monitoring 7,000 miles of shared borders with Mexico and Canada, 95,000 miles of shoreline, and 329 ports of entry. Even with a workforce of 60,000, CBP met just 73 percent of requests for its air assets in fiscal year 2010—the goal is 95 percent—due to the lack of maintenance for aging aircraft, insufficient all-weather planes, and understaffing, according to the GAO. Surveillance drones offer the CBP a number of advantages over manned aircraft, such as longer mission duration over remote areas, while providing near real-time imagery via video cameras and thermal infrared and synthetic aperture radars.

Although variants of the Predator are configured to carry armed missiles, it is important to note that CBP drones will not bomb U.S. citizens. There is a common misperception, perpetuated by the media, that all drones drop bombs. But less than 4 percent of the Pentagon's 6,316 drones, for instance, are armed and capable of conducting strike missions. And in a voice vote regarding DHS funding on June 7, the House of Representatives stipulated: "None of the funds made available by this Act may be used for the purchase, operation, or maintenance of armed unmanned aerial vehicles."

The good news about domestic drones is that . . . there is a great deal of publicly available information detailing their bases, operational command and control, missions, and costs.

The primary issue with CBP drones is not that they are used, but *how* they are used—specifically, that drones are rushed into the field before the requisite framework, plans, and resources are fully developed. A report released by the DHS inspector general in May found that "CBP procured unmanned aircraft before implementing adequate plans to do the following: achieve the desired level of operation; acquire sufficient funding to provide necessary operations, maintenance, and equipment; and coordinate and support stakeholder needs." At the same time, CBP Predator B drones cost more than three times more to fly per hour than their Department of Defense counterparts. Despite the high costs, some members of Congress—specifically the 58-member Congressional Unmanned Systems Caucus—continue to push drones on the CBP. Last fall, Congress appropriated $32 million to the CBP to purchase three additional Predator drones, after which a CBP official acknowledged, "We didn't ask for them."

As a result, CBP drones have had limited success in the field so far. In 2011, CBP drones helped to locate 7,600 pounds of marijuana, valued at a paltry $19 million. Drones also reportedly laid the groundwork for the apprehension of 4,865 undocumented immigrants between 2006 and 2011—an underwhelming statistic considering that a total of 327,577 people were captured in 2011 alone.

The good news about domestic drones is that, unlike the "covert" missions conducted abroad by the Pentagon and CIA, there is a great deal of publicly available information detailing their bases, operational command and control, missions, and costs. And, in contrast to media portrayals, domestic drones used for CBP missions enjoy measured support among U.S. citizens. In a recent poll, 64 percent of respondents approved of the use of drones "to control illegal immigration on the nation's border," and 80 percent "to help with search and rescue missions." (Sixty-seven percent were opposed to drones enforcing speed limits—even though manned aircraft already perform this function in 19 states across the country.)

If properly planned for and funded, drones can play a critical, niche role in monitoring U.S. borders. But if there is anything to be learned from America's use of drones abroad, it is that mission creep follows. Once security forces have access to the near real-time video and radar surveillance that drones can provide, they become addicted—and subsequently develop new missions for how drones can be used. This is the reason that, in order to assure the protection of privacy and civil liberties, there must be rigorous, sustained, and effective oversight by Congress and the courts of all drones in the United States.

12

Drones Are Effective for Border Security and Disaster Assistance

Michael C. Kostelnik

Michael C. Kostelnik, a retired major general of the United States Air Force, is the assistant commissioner for the Office of Air and Marine within US Customs and Border Protection.

The US Customs and Border Protection (CBP), a part of the Department of Homeland Security, uses drones to protect America's borders, reduce the flow of drugs into the United States, and respond to natural and manmade disasters. Drones have several advantages as a homeland security tool: they can provide over twenty hours of surveillance on one mission and carry sensors to meet evolving threats. Drones can also be adapted to conduct maritime surveillance and drug interception missions. In fact, the Federal Aviation Administration has approved drones, as they can operate safely in national airspace systems. Indeed, congressional support for domestic drones will help the CBP continue its homeland security mission.

It is a privilege and an honor to appear before you [the House Committee on Homeland Security, Subcommittee on Border, Maritime, and Global Counterterrorism] today to discuss the employment of the Predator B and Guardian Unmanned Aircraft System (UAS) for homeland security mis-

Michael C. Kostelnik, "The Role of Unmanned Aircraft Systems in Border Security," Testimony Before the House Committee on Homeland Security, Subcommittee on Border, Maritime, and Global Counterterrorism, July 15, 2010.

sions by U.S. Customs and Border Protection's (CBP) Office of Air and Marine (OAM), and in particular their role in border security operations. I want to begin by expressing my gratitude to the Committee for its continuing support of the CBP mission, especially as it relates to our efforts to expand UAS operations over both the land and maritime borders of the United States.

CBP has operated the Predator B UAS for over five years and has pioneered the employment of this high-end, long duration, remotely-piloted aircraft in the National Airspace System (NAS) for border security and disaster assistance. Predator Bs, which can operate in excess of 20 hours during a single border search mission, currently patrol parts of both the southern and northern U.S. land borders and have logged more than 6,500 flight hours in support of CBP's border security mission. The newest addition to CBP's UAS family, a maritime search variant of the Predator B called the Guardian, carries a broad-area sea-search radar with impressive long range detection and tracking capabilities. Together, the Guardian and Predator B have enabled CBP to support the response to large-scale natural events such as hurricanes, floods, and the oil spill in the Gulf of Mexico;[1] and have positioned CBP to confront ever-changing threats to the homeland in the future.

Current Operations and Deployment Strategy

CBP currently operates six Predator B aircraft, including the first maritime Guardian which was developed under a joint program office with the United States Coast Guard (USCG). A seventh aircraft, our second Guardian, is scheduled for deliv-

---

1. The author refers to the April 20, 2010, Deepwater Horizon explosion that spilled oil into the Gulf of Mexico. The explosion claimed eleven lives and resulted in a three-month, unabated flow of oil into the Gulf and led to significant environmental and economic damage. The total discharge is estimated at 4.9 million barrels.

ery before the end of this year [2010], and funding for a third Guardian is included in the President's Fiscal Year (FY) 2011 Budget request. The Predator family of aircraft has an evolving sensor suite and has flown over one million hours on defense missions. The CBP version of the aircraft has a 66 foot wing span and weighs over 10,000 pounds. Since 2005, the main operating base for the UAS has been the U.S. Army's Fort Huachuca, located near Sierra Vista, AZ. CBP has three Predators deployed to Sierra Vista to conduct missions along the southwest border, and to develop tactics, test new sensors, and train new pilots and sensor operators. Since the UAS is designated by CBP as a national asset, broad operations are directed from OAM National Air Security Operations Office (NASO) in Washington, DC. Individual mission assignments are generally based on specific intelligence, intelligence trends, and requests from the CBP Field Commanders at the southwest and northern borders. Other Department of Homeland Security (DHS) component agencies, such as the Federal Emergency Management Agency (FEMA) and the USCG, as well as outside federal agencies, such as the FBI and DEA, also make requests.

[Drones] can be flown safely in the NAS [National Airspace System], with operational limitations that ensure the safety of other NAS users and people and property on the ground.

In December 2008, CBP deployed its first Predator B to North Dakota to commence northern border operations and enhance pilot training opportunities. By February 2009, two aircraft were operating from Grand Forks Air Force Base, North Dakota. In the fall and winter of 2008 to 2009, CBP Predators drawn from both the northern and southern borders supported FEMA missions during the southeastern hurricanes and the floods in North Dakota. During the hurricane activity, the Predators conducted pre- and post-event missions that mapped 260 critical infrastructure points of interest and provided FEMA and the Army Corps of Engineers vital video and change detection information on storm damage. During the North Dakota and Midwest floods of 2009, the aircraft flew nearly 100 hours during 11 missions, and provided video on the formation of ice dams so that action could be taken to destroy them and prevent the floods from expanding.

Cooperative Operations

CBP and the USCG began cooperating on UAS operations in 2007, beginning with a UAS rapid deployment demonstration to North Dakota named *Agile Falcon*. Using a USCG C-130 cargo aircraft, a complete system including the Predator B support equipment and ground control station was successfully airlifted, proving the capability that will eventually be used to support the introduction of the Guardian into the eastern Pacific drug transit zone. In March 2008, the USCG participated in a CBP-led demonstration of a maritime UAS capability off Tyndall Air Force Base, Florida. And in the months that followed, the USCG joined CBP in the creation of a Joint Program Office for the development of a maritime Predator variant.

On the heels of a highly successful partnership with the North Dakota Air National Guard, CBP aggressively sought to expand operations to the eastern half of the northern border. In June 2009, OAM conducted a successful surge operation to the Great Lakes and St. Lawrence Seaway, operating from the Army's Wheeler-Sack air field at Fort Drum, New York. The air field at Fort Drum is perfectly located to support routine UAS operations along the northern maritime border, as well as contingency operations along the eastern seaboard. OAM also began work on a long-range partnership with the New York Air National Guard's 174th Fighter Wing (FW) in Syracuse, New York, to share maintenance, training, and logistic support common to CBP Predators. The 174th FW also possesses the capability to support CBP UAS operations, either from Wheeler-Sack Army Air Field at Fort Drum, or directly from Hancock Field in Syracuse.

> *Eventually, [the Guardian drone] is expected to be deployed alongside the P-3 patrol aircraft, searching for bulk drug carriers, such as semi-submersible vessels and bulk drug submarines.*

Access to the National Airspace System (NAS)

The Predator B and Guardian are two high-end, remotely-piloted unmanned aircraft routinely operating in the NAS under Certificates of Authorization (COAs) from the Federal Aviation Administration (FAA). CBP has worked with the FAA to meet all requirements of its COA application process and the detailed, tailored requirements of individual certificates. OAM has demonstrated that the Predator B can be flown safely in the NAS, with operational limitations that ensure the safety of other NAS users and people and property on the ground. It is a proven operational system with redundant command and control, under the operational oversight of the Air and Marine Operations Center (AMOC), and the flight safety oversight of the FAA. It is flown along the nation's borders and coastlines, primarily at night when civilian air traffic is low, and it is flown in support of critical national security missions. To date, 35 of 36 COA requests made by CBP have been approved by the FAA. The latest COA approvals have increased the miles of airspace available for UAS operations, including 1,103 miles above Texas, enabling CBP to deploy its unmanned aircraft from the eastern tip of California, across the land borders of Arizona, New Mexico, and Texas, and into the maritime border just short of the Texas and

Louisiana border. The other recent COA approval granted access to airspace needed to deploy the Guardian UAS, and a Predator B temporarily re-deployed from North Dakota, over the Deepwater Horizon oil spill. CBP continues to work with the FAA to expand access from 240 to over 900 miles along the northern border, west of North Dakota, and then, as resources permit, back to the Great Lakes and St. Lawrence Seaway. The FAA has assured CBP that homeland security COA requests will be given top priority.

Expanding into the Maritime Domain

Work on a maritime variant of the Predator B began in late 2007 and the path forward to the new capability took shape after the UAS Maritime Demonstration conducted in March 2008. By November 2008, CBP and the USCG had signed a charter for the Joint Program Office. Within a few months thereafter, modification of an existing Predator B as the first prototype Guardian began and the completed aircraft was delivered to CBP in December 2009. The Guardian's primary enhancement was the addition of a SeaVue broad-area maritime search radar, common to the radars being flown on CBP's P-3 long-range tracker aircraft and the DHC-8 medium range patrol aircraft. Other enhancements included electro-optical/infrared sensors with maritime haze filters, a 360-degree maritime automatic information system (AIS), and an upgraded power subsystem with twice the output of a standard Predator B.

The Guardian maritime UAS successfully completed operations test and evaluation in May 2010, and the early results indicate that it will provide DHS with an impressive capability for maritime surveillance and interdiction missions in the source and transit zones. The aircraft is currently deployed to Canaveral Air Force Station, Florida, and is an additional asset in use with the unified response command assisting with the BP Deepwater Horizon oil spill. Plans are in place for embarking on the first joint CBP/USCG mission in the Caribbean Sea later this summer. Eventually, the aircraft is expected to be deployed alongside the P-3 patrol aircraft, searching for bulk drug carriers, such as semi-submersible vessels and bulk drug submarines, in the Caribbean and eastern Pacific. Less than one year after the selection of a radar system, CBP introduced a unique, long-range maritime search asset to the DHS inventory, unmatched by any other capability on the world stage.

No other [Customs and Border Protection] aircraft can provide persistent surveillance for over 20 hours in a single mission ... and host a variety of sensors to meet the evolving threat on the land and maritime borders.

Future Plans

When DHS approved the UAS Program as a component of CBP's Strategic Air and Marine Plan (StAMP), OAM was authorized to acquire up to 24 complete systems. Consistent with the available resources, OAM has acquired seven aircraft, including five Predator B land configuration aircraft and two maritime Guardians. As previously stated, the FY 2011 budget request includes funding for an eighth aircraft, also a Guardian. To support the aircraft, their command and control systems, operations personnel, maintenance and logistics, and other infrastructure, OAM established three launch, landing, and mission control sites (Sierra Vista, Arizona; Grand Forks, North Dakota; and Cape Canaveral, Florida), along with a mission operations site at the AMOC.

To further bolster our southwest border security resources, CBP re-deployed a ground control station from the AMOC to the Naval Air Station, Corpus Christi, Texas this month. Current plans call for occasional surge operations to Corpus Christi until sufficient aircraft, crew, ground support equipment, and operating funds become available, and a launch site agreement is reached with the U.S. Navy. Since the approval of the FAA COA for southern Texas and Corpus Christi, CBP has made steady progress on a basing agreement. With aircraft launched from both Sierra Vista, Arizona, and Corpus Christi, Texas, CBP can cover the full length of the 1,185 miles of airspace approved for homeland security operations by the FAA.

Enhancing Homeland Security Missions

CBP UAS operations provide leading edge capabilities to homeland security missions. No other CBP aircraft can provide persistent surveillance for over 20 hours in a single mission, respond to urgent calls from ground agents for unparalleled situational awareness, and host a variety of sensors to meet the evolving threat on the land and maritime borders.

Over the past three years, CBP has established formal relationships with the Department of Defense (DOD) and its components to leverage capabilities developed for use overseas that may have applications to homeland security missions. The capabilities fall into three broad categories: sensor systems; video and data capture and exploitation systems; and hardware support. Since OAM is an operating organization with minimal research and development staff or supporting test and evaluation infrastructure, it is logical and efficient to take advantage of technological advances by the DOD, industry, and other agencies.

I would like to highlight three specific DOD capabilities that are being tested or adopted by CBP to enhance UAS performance for homeland security. The first would provide CBP with a radar capability with active, near-real time vehicle and dismounted change detection, to support border ground operations, especially in areas subject to high levels of border violence. Once proven on the Predator, the capability could be distributed to other CBP surveillance aircraft. The second capability would provide enhanced signals direction-finding capabilities that could be used both over land and during coastal and long range maritime operations. A third capability, funded by Congress in FY 2010, will provide infrastructure for the timely exploitation of information and video from a variety of aviation platforms and sensors, beginning with the UAS and P-3 long range patrol aircraft. Exploitation can be defined as the detailed analysis, interpretation, and distribution of information from many sources; eventually this will provide a nationwide capability to coordinate aviation mission assignments during broad border area campaigns and major events. Located at the AMOC, the first processing, exploitation, and dissemination cell is being patterned after similar capabilities employed by the U.S. Air Force and is expected to be operational before the end of this year.

The Road Ahead

No aviation program, no matter how effective and efficient, is without challenges. The greatest near-term challenge faced by CBP's UAS Program is a shortage of pilots and sensor operators, specifically pilots certified to launch and land the aircraft. There is a significant amount of competition among the DOD, industry, and DHS to hire UAS pilots. Last year, Congress provided funds for 24 new pilots and though all were hired, only a few brought with them significant UAS experience. The rest are undergoing training that will take the better part of this year to complete. CBP does not plan to hire additional UAS pilots in FY 2011, except to cover retirements, and therefore has begun to cross-train pilots and sensor operators from other high-in-demand units, primarily those stationed at the CBP P-3 branch in Corpus Christi. Since CBP plans to operate Predators and Guardians from Corpus Christi, it is logical and efficient to share resources to the maximum extent possible.

As previously mentioned, CBP continues to work very closely with the FAA on UAS access to the NAS, with the objective of eventually establishing long-term or permanent corridors through which CBP can routinely fly missions along the nation's land and coastal borders, into the source and transit zones, and respond to emergency missions across the country. The relatively recent establishment of a UAS Executive Committee that includes DHS, FAA, DOD, and the National Aeronautics and Space Administration, will help to address government-wide NAS access needs. Since CBP has a homeland security mission in the NAS, the agency's COA requests will receive top priority by the FAA.

Mr. Chairman and Members of the Subcommittee, thank you for this opportunity to testify about the work of U.S. Customs and Border Protection, particularly in regard to the impressive capabilities that unmanned aircraft systems bring to our homeland security missions. Your continued support of CBP and the UAS program has led to significant improvements in the security of our borders and our nation.

13

The Ability of Drones to Secure America's Borders Remains Unproven

Brian Bennett

Brian Bennett is the national security correspondent in Washington, DC, for the Los Angeles Times *newspaper.*

Drones have not yet demonstrated that they are a useful border security tool. Drones require a great deal of maintenance and cannot operate in bad weather. In truth, a homeland security audit revealed that the US Customs and Border Protection drone fleet flew only half of its scheduled hours. Indeed, drones provide mixed results. While drones can identify drug smuggling activity, for example, they cannot respond. Nevertheless, border patrol officials see the potential of these unmanned aerial vehicles. Drones can in fact observe and report when border security personnel may be in danger.

The drug runners call it "*el mosco*," the mosquito, and one recent evening on the southern tip of Texas, a Predator B drone armed with cameras buzzed softly over the beach on South Padre Island and headed inland.

A Domestic Drone Story

"We're going to get some bad guys tonight, I've got a feeling," said Scott Peterson, a U.S. Customs and Border Protection supervisory air interdiction agent. He watched the drone's live video feed in the Predator Ops room at Naval Air Station Corpus Christi, about 50 miles away.

As the unmanned plane flew up the winding Rio Grande, which forms the border with Mexico, Peterson fielded excited phone calls. One agent had seen known scouts for a Mexican cartel at a Dairy Queen, suggesting a load of drugs was coming through. Another called in the precise spot where the shipment would land.

Soon the drone's infrared camera picked up a man hauling bales of marijuana from an inflatable rubber boat into a minivan on the Texas side of the river. Then it spotted a second boat. Agents readied for a major bust.

But the April 18 [2012] raid was not the success Peterson had envisioned. He wanted the drone to track the smugglers to a stash house, and perhaps to ranking cartel members. Instead, Border Patrol agents rushed to the riverbank, sirens blaring. They seized half a ton of pot, a 1996 Plymouth Voyager van and a boat. The smugglers escaped and no one was arrested.

Mixed Results

The mixed results highlight a glaring problem for Homeland Security officials who have spent six years and more than $250 million building the nation's largest fleet of domestic surveillance drones: The nine Predators that help police America's borders have yet to prove very useful in stopping contraband or illegal immigrants.

The border drones require an hour of maintenance for every hour they fly, cost more to operate than anticipated, and are frequently grounded by rain or other bad weather, according to a draft audit of the program last month by the Homeland Security Department's inspector general.

Last year, the unmanned fleet flew barely half the number of flight hours that Customs and Border Protection had scheduled on the northern or southern borders, or over the Caribbean, according to the audit.

And the drones often are unavailable to assist border agents because Homeland Security officials have lent the aircraft to the FBI, Texas Rangers and other government agencies for law enforcement, disaster relief and other uses.

The amount of illicit drugs seized in Predator [drone] raids is "not impressive."

The audit slammed Homeland Security for buying two drones last year and ordering an additional $20.5-million Predator B system in Cocoa Beach, Fla., this year, saying it already owns more drones than it can utilize. Each drone costs about $3,000 an hour to fly.

"The big problem is that they are more expensive than traditional methods" of patrolling, said T.J. Bonner, former president of the National Border Patrol Council, a union of border agents.

To help pay for the drones, Customs and Border Protection has raided budgets of its manned aircraft. One result: Flight hours were cut by 10% for the P-3 Orion maritime surveillance planes that hunt smuggling ships on the West Coast and in the Caribbean.

An Unimpressive Record

The amount of illicit drugs seized in Predator raids is "not impressive," acknowledged Michael Kostelnik, a retired Air Force major general who heads the office that supervises the drones.

Last year, the nine border drones helped find 7,600 pounds of marijuana, valued at $19.3 million. The 14 manned P-3 Orions helped intercept 148,000 pounds of cocaine valued at $2.8 billion.

In an interview, Kostelnik dismissed criticism of the border drones as shortsighted. He sketched out scenarios, such as a nuclear plant meltdown or detonation of a dirty bomb, where the drones could help assess damage without endangering a pilot.

If a major terrorist attack occurred in Washington or New York City, Kostelnik said, he could put drones overhead in five hours, assuming they could be flown up from Florida or carried on a cargo plane, to help first responders and policymakers.

"It is not about the things we are doing today," Kostelnik said. "It is about the things we might be able to do."

Border Drone Pros and Cons

The recent raid on the Rio Grande showed some of the pros and cons of the border drones.

Inside the Predator Ops center, the crew watched as the minivan filled with marijuana drove away on a dirt road. The Predator's camera followed. Suddenly, a figure raced in front of the minivan, waving his hands for the driver to turn back.

"He's spooked!" said Lyle Belew, the mission commander. "Stay on him!" he ordered the camera operator as the van did a quick U-turn.

Instead of risking a potentially violent standoff in a nearby residential neighborhood, the agents on the ground decided to cut the operation short and try to seize the drugs at the river.

A Border Patrol SUV suddenly appeared on screen, chasing the minivan back to the riverbank. Then six figures jumped out of the minivan and into the water, taking one of the two rubber boats. Several Border Patrol agents ran down the beach in pursuit.

In the Ops Center, Border Patrol liaison Hector Black worried that cartel gunmen might open fire on his agents from the far side of the river.

"Ask them to pan [the drone camera] to Mexico to make sure nobody starts shooting at our guys," Black said. "See if there are guys with long arms," meaning rifles.

The banks looked empty, but the camera clearly showed six figures and a rubber boat drifting down the dark river and back into Mexico.

14

Drones Are an Effective Environmental Protection Tool

Denis D. Gray

Denis D. Gray is a journalist with the Associated Press who covers issues concerning Southeast Asia.

Conservationists and activists use drones as an environmental protection tool. For example, conservationists can track wildlife, identify poachers, and map where forests are being cleared. Antiwhaling activists use drones to photograph Japanese whaling vessels, which improves efforts to block these ships. One of the greatest advantages of drones is that tracking wildlife in rugged terrain or at sea is easier from the air. Indeed, conservationists from the University of Florida have plans to use drones in the United States to track wildlife in remote locations. Although conservation drones are not as sophisticated as US military drones, they are a useful part of broad conservation efforts.

They're better known as stealthy killing machines to take out suspected terrorists with pinpoint accuracy. But drones are also being put to more benign use in skies across several continents to track endangered wildlife, spot poachers and chart forest loss.

Although it's still the "dawn of drone ecology," as one innovator calls it, these unmanned aerial vehicles are already skimming over Indonesia's jungle canopy to photograph orangutans, protecting rhinos in Nepal and studying invasive aquatic plants in Florida.

Activists launched a long-range drone in December [2011] to locate and photograph a Japanese whaling ship as the Sea Shepherd Conservation Society attempted to block Japan's annual whale hunt in Antarctic waters. Relatively cheap, portable and earth-hugging, they fill a gap between satellite and manned aircraft imagery and on-the-ground observations, says Percival Franklin at the University of Florida, which has been developing such drones for more than a decade.

"The potential uses are almost unlimited," says Ian Singleton, director of the Sumatran Orangutan Conservation Program, testing drones this year over Indonesia's Tripa peat forest where fires set by palm oil growers are threatening the world's highest density habitat of the great apes.

Drones . . . provide high-resolution, real-time images showing where forests are being cleared and set ablaze.

Useful for Dull, Dirty or Dangerous Jobs

Conservation is one of the latest roles for these multi-taskers, either autonomously controlled by on-board computers or under remote guidance of a navigator. Ranging in size from less than half a kilogram (pound) to more than 18 metric tons (20 tons), drones have been used for firefighting, road patrols, hurricane tracking and other jobs too dull, dirty or dangerous for piloted craft.

Most prominently, they have been harnessed by the U.S. military in recent years, often to detect and kill opponents in America's "war on terror" in Afghanistan, Pakistan and elsewhere.

A conservation drone pioneer, Lian Pin Koh of the Swiss Federal Institute of Technology, says the idea came to him after another sweaty, jungle slog in Sabah, Malaysia, hauling heavy equipment for his field work.

"I told my assistant, who happened to be my wife, 'How wonderful it would be if we could fly over that area rather than walk there again tomorrow,'" recalled the Singaporean expert on tropical deforestation, and a model plane hobbyist.

Unlike eco-drones in the United States, mostly custom-built or commercial models, Koh last year cobbled together a far cheaper, off-the-shelf version that poorer organizations and governments in the developing world can better afford.

He and partner Serge Wich bought a model plane—some are available in China for as little as $100—added an autopilot system, open source software to program missions, and still and video cameras. All for less than $2,000, or ten times cheaper than some commercial vehicles with similar capabilities.

This year, they have flown more than 200 mostly test runs in Asia using an improved version with a 2-meter (6.5 foot) wing span, air time of 45 minutes and a 25-kilometer (15.5-mile) range.

The drones were flown over rough terrain in Malaysia where GPS-collared elephants are difficult to monitor from the ground. In Nepal's Chitwan National Park, the World Wide Fund for Nature (WWF) and the Nepal Army conducted trials on detecting rhino and elephant poachers. The duo also assisted the Ugalla Primate Project to head count chimpanzees in western Tanzania. "Counting orangutan nests is the main way of surveying orangutan populations," says Graham Usher of the Sumatran project, which captured one of the apes atop a palm tree feeding on palm heart in a sharp photograph. From higher altitudes the drones, he said, also provide high-resolution, real-time images showing where forests are being cleared and set ablaze.

More Efficient than Ground Expeditions

By contrast ground expeditions are time-consuming, logistically cumbersome and expensive. A conventional orangutan census in Sumatra, which may also involve helicopters and aircraft, costs some $250,000. Surveying land use by satellite is likewise costly and hampered by frequent cloud cover over tropical areas.

But there are drawbacks with drones, including landing them in often thickly vegetated areas since they need clear touch-down zones of about 100 by 100 meters (yards). Koh said he was working to rig the vehicle with a parachute to allow landing in confined space.

Franklin says the hardware and image interpretation are still being developed as more missions are planned in the United States, ranging from counting pygmy rabbit burrows in Idaho to monitoring salmon-eating seabirds off the Oregon coast.

The University of Florida is testing another "war on terror" weapon, thermal imaging, to hunt for Burmese pythons invading the state's Everglades, having found the snakes regulate temperatures of their nests in a way that makes them visible through such technology.

Other Conservation Surveillance Tools

Other eyes-in-the-sky increasingly used for conservation tasks are ultralights, birdlike craft with a major advantage over drones—the human touch.

"It's the closest thing we have come to flying like birds 30,000 years after coming out of caves," says Mark Silverberg, preparing to take a reporter up in a para-motor ultralight, one earlier hired by conservation groups to photograph and video Mekong River dolphins, tiger habitat in Myanmar and denuded hills in northern Thailand.

Taking off from a fallow rice field in Pranburi district, south of the Thai capital Bangkok, we nearly brush branches as our two-seater ultralight craft needles through stands of trees, follows a flock of waterfowl just below us, then soars to 300 meters (980 feet) for an all-horizons view. Where humanity intersects with nature is clearly evident, and beyond loom limestone cliffs of a national park invaded by polluting shrimp farms.

"I can really craft a shoot, a sequence, show scenes better than drones because there is a human being who can take in and react to the whole environment more immediately and make adjustments," says Silverberg, an American who runs Paramotor Thailand.

The ultralight, he explains, has other advantages over most eco-drones: it can remain airborne for up to 3 hours, cover 70 kilometers (43 miles) and carry heavier payloads. But ultralights are rather noisy and pilots are reluctant to fly over water or thick vegetation in event of an emergency landing.

"All in all, there's really no competition with drones," says Silverberg after the flight over south of Bangkok. "Both are really great tools for conservation."

15

A Drone Industry Code of Conduct Is Inadequate to Protect Americans

Peter W. Singer and Jeffrey Lin

Peter W. Singer is director of the Center for 21st Century Security and Intelligence at the Brookings Institution, where Jeffrey Lin is an intern. Singer is also the author of Wired for War: The Robotics Revolution and Conflict in the 21st Century.

When the public expressed outrage and fear upon learning that drones would be used in US airspace, the drone industry responded by issuing its own code of conduct. While a positive first step, the code has no real consequences for failure to meet code standards. Vague promises to respect privacy and employ only well-trained personal are subject to broad interpretation. The code also ignores how the industry will keep drone technology from those who would abuse it. Promises to follow the law make for good sound bites, but in the end such promises say more about the need for laws than the effectiveness of a code of conduct.

The last several months [May–July 2012] were supposed to be good times for the makers of unmanned aerial systems, popularly known as "drones." Business is booming and theirs is one of the few parts of the aerospace industry not shaking in its boots at impending defense budget cuts. And the $2.3 million spent on lobbying Congress finally seems to

Peter W. Singer and Jeffrey Lin, "Baby Steps: The Drone Industry's Code of Conduct Skips over Key Questions," *The Atlantic*, July 19, 2012. Reproduced by permission.

have paid off. In February [2012], Congress ordered the FAA [Federal Aviation Administration] to figure out an action plan to open up the national air space to unmanned systems (currently, only those with special agreements, such as for Border Patrol, are allowed) by 2015, as well as set up six experimentation locales.

This will put an already strong business on steroids, akin to what the development of the Internet did for the computer industry. Rather than just selling to the Pentagon, the new clients might range from the more than 21,000 state and local law enforcement departments to farmers, journalists, and more, as they find new and innovative uses for unmanned systems, from overhead surveillance to crop-dusting.

A Public Relations Nightmare

The problem is that what appeared to be good news for the industry instead turned into a public-relations nightmare. Both left and right came together in condemnation and worry over the implications of this move, especially on privacy rights. Perhaps the most extreme example was when Charles Krauthammer, the right-wing columnist and Fox News commentator, reacted to the news by saying, "I'm going to go hard left on you here, I'm going ACLU [American Civil Liberties Union]" and calling for an absolute ban: "I don't want regulations, I don't want restrictions, I want a ban on this." He then swung back to the traditional right, adding, "The first guy who uses a Second Amendment weapon to bring a drone down that's been hovering over his house is going to be a folk hero in this country."

Even worse for the industry, policymakers began to take seriously some of the stories about drones run amok that went viral on the Internet. Some of those stories turned out to be false, such as when Nebraska's congressional delegation complained to the EPA about federal government drones illegally "spying" on farmers, despite the story having no factual basis. Soon, legislators at the state and federal levels were racing to submit bills to roll back the planned domestic drone boom.

An Industry Code of Conduct

Faced with the backlash, the trade group for the industry, the Association for Unmanned Vehicles Systems International (AUVSI), which had originally taken credit for literally writing the exact language used in the FAA bill, tried to stem the bleeding with a classic move from the bad-press playbook. Last week, it issued an industry "code of conduct."

> *Like such other would-be "codes of conduct," [the drone industry code of conduct] lacks one key ingredient: consequences.*

That move was a positive step, showing that the industry finally recognizes that drones have great potential to the nation (and great potential for profits as well), but only if they successfully navigate the deep concerns that the technology evokes. The code smartly discussed how "as with every revolutionary technology, there will be mishaps and abuses," but that the key to winning "public acceptance and trust" is openness and transparency. This would seem to be common sense, but it's a new turn for an industry that has largely been Pollyannaish about public concerns. Just a few years ago, a survey of AUVSI key stakeholders found that 60 percent believed that there would be "no" social, ethical, or moral problems to emerge from the advancement of unmanned systems.

Changing course, the code of conduct took on many of the concerns circulating, grouping them into three core themes of Safety, Professionalism, and Respect. It laid out how the industry and users would "commit" to not operating drones "in a manner that presents undue risk to persons or property;" to planning for "all anticipated off-nominal events;" and to share such contingency plans with "all appropriate authorities." It made great sense and was reported widely.

A Lack of Consequences

The challenge for the robotics code of conduct is much the same as other industries' attempts at self-regulation, ranging from banking to the private military industry. It's a laudable start, but it doesn't change the underlying issues and concerns. Like such other would-be "codes of conduct," it lacks one key ingredient: consequences.

Despite purporting to cover "those who design, test and operate UAS [unmanned aircraft systems]," [the drone industry code of conduct] avoids stating any specific intent or concern about those we'd rather not see be involved in the field.

As it stands now, the golfer who violates his country club's code of conduct risks stiffer punishments than a drone maker or user who violates the terms of their new code. Golfers might lose a point, or even be kicked out the club, if they violate their agreement. The new robotics code doesn't include a single potential sanction, such as, for example, something like kicking violators out of the trade group. Indeed, much of what is laid out is actually restatements of responsibilities the firms and users already must abide by, regardless of any code. For example, the code says that the firms "will comply with all federal, state and local laws." So, before the code, they could violate the law at will? Of course not. Saying one will follow the law is one of those things that sounds meaningful but is ultimately meaningless, as it just illustrates the importance of the law, not the code.

Similarly, the code is quite vague on a variety of legitimate concerns. It says that "we will ensure that UAS [unmanned aircraft systems] are piloted by individuals who are properly trained and competent to operate the vehicle or its systems." Who will determine this, and what does "trained and competent" mean in a world where some believe drones should only be operated by rated pilots, even though new versions can be flown by teens using iPhone apps? Likewise, the code pledges to "respect the privacy of individuals," which is a bold statement with nothing about what it actually means. "Respect" could be anything from avoiding the monitoring of individuals without their express permission to showing them "respect" only in the public-relations sense.

Thorny Issues

Of course, these are thorny issues. Indeed, it's their very thorniness that is why an industry self-regulatory code—especially one that emerged in the context of bad press and built around lowest common denominator agreement within a trade group—would sensibly want to avoid them for now. But the irony is that resolving these problems is what actually matters to the industry's overall goal of "gaining public trust and acceptance." The same need for resolution goes for the pressing concerns that the code completely ignored. For example, despite purporting to cover "those who design, test and operate UAS," it avoids stating any specific intent or concern about those we'd rather not see be involved in the field. What can we do not just to promote a powerful technology for good, but also to stop the illicit use by or unintended transfer of the technology to dangerous actors? Much like the technology, such worries are not science fiction. Everyone from terrorists to jewelry thieves to vigilante groups have already used UAS technology.

Likewise, while the code outlines how weather conditions and other potential causes of accidents are to be included in risk assessments, there is no mention in the Safety section on whether or how the industry might work to address hostile man-made threats, including criminal or adversarial efforts at

UAS communications interference or hacking. Here again, this scenario is not science fiction, but was recently demonstrated in a test in Texas, where a university team hacked the navigation system of a drone. Part of the absence may be explained by another omission. How does the code view potential responsibilities (and hence liabilities) against its members in the event of "off-nominal" events it now believes are possible?

As with revolutionary inventions of the past, like the horseless carriage and manned airplanes, no amount of handwringing by pundits late to the game will see a technology of such great promise banned. That said, new technologies bring with them the need for revising old laws. Early cars and planes, for instance, led to the creation of newfangled things like "traffic laws" and the Federal Aviation Administration. The drone industry's code of conduct points toward key issues that effort will have to tackle, so it must be viewed as something more than just public relations. But it also shows the long way we have to go in establishing actual policy and real laws.

16

Legal Safeguards Are Needed to Protect Against Domestic Use of Drones

Amie Stepanovich

Amie Stepanovich is association litigation counsel for the Electronic Privacy Information Center, an advocacy organization and think tank that focuses on privacy and civil liberties concerns surrounding electronic technologies.

Although drones clearly have the potential to serve and protect American citizens, current laws are inadequate to protect privacy. Because law enforcement agencies will use drones to monitor Americans in broad new ways, Congress must develop privacy laws and policies that specifically address this new technology. Indeed, activist organizations and privacy experts recommend that lawmakers establish privacy safeguards before drones become more widely deployed. Law enforcement should use drones only under very specific circumstances and only when they have obtained a judicial warrant. In addition, lawmakers must place strict limitations on how law enforcement shares the data acquired by drones. Finally, strict oversight of drone surveillance operations is crucial.

Thank you for the opportunity to testify today concerning unmanned aerial systems, or drones, in the United States. My name is Amie Stepanovich. I am the Associate Litigation Counsel at the Electronic Privacy Information Center.

Amie Stepanovich, Hearing on "Using Unmanned Aerial Systems Within the Homeland: Security Game Changer?," Testimony and Statement for the Record Before the Subcommittee on Oversight, Investigations, and Management of the US House of Representatives Committee on Homeland Security, July 19, 2012.

EPIC is a non-partisan research organization, established in 1994, to focus public attention on emerging privacy and civil liberties issues. We work with a distinguished panel of advisors in the fields of law, technology, and public policy. We have a particular interest in the protection of individual privacy rights against government surveillance. In the last several years, EPIC has taken a particular interest in the unique privacy problems associated with aerial drones. We have urged the Federal Aviation Administration ("FAA"), as it considers new regulations to permit the widespread deployment of drones, to also develop new privacy safeguards.

In my statement today, I will describe the unique threats to privacy posed by drone surveillance, the problems with current legal safeguards, the EPIC petition to the FAA, and the need for Congress to act.

We appreciate the Subcommittee's interest in domestic drone use and its substantial impact on the privacy of individuals in the United States.

Aerial Drones Pose a Unique Threat to Privacy

An unmanned aircraft, or drone, is an aerial vehicle designed to fly without a human pilot on board. Drones can either be remotely controlled or autonomous. Drones can be weaponized and deployed for military purposes. Drones can also be equipped with sophisticated surveillance technology that makes it possible to identify individuals on the ground. Gigapixel cameras used to outfit drones are among the highest definition cameras available, and can provide "real-time video streams at a rate of 10 frames a second." On some drones, sensors can track up to 65 different targets across a distance of 65 square miles. Drones may also carry infrared cameras, heat sensors, GPS, sensors that detect movement, and automated license plate readers. Drones are currently being developed that will carry facial recognition technology, able to remotely identify individuals in parks, schools, and at political gatherings.

In a report on drones published by EPIC in 2005, we observed, "the use of [drones] gives the federal government a new capability to monitor citizens clandestinely, while the effectiveness of the . . . surveillance planes in border patrol operations has not been proved." Today, drones greatly increase the capacity for domestic surveillance.

Sensitive information collected by drones is particularly vulnerable to unlawful access.

Much of this surveillance technology could, in theory, be deployed in manned vehicles. However, drones present a unique threat to privacy. Drones are designed to undertake constant, persistent surveillance to a degree that former methods of surveillance were unable to achieve. Drones are cheaper to buy, maintain, and operate than helicopters, or other forms of aerial surveillance. Drone manufacturers have recently announced new designs that would allow drones to operate for more than 48 consecutive hours, and other technology could extend the flight time of future drones out into weeks and months. Also, "by virtue of their design, size, and how high they can fly, [drones] can operate undetected in urban and rural environments."

The ability to link facial recognition capabilities on drones operated by the Department of Homeland Security ("DHS") to the Federal Bureau of Investigation's Next Generation Identification database or DHS' IDENT database, two of the largest collections of biometric data in the world, exacerbates the privacy risks. Drones could be deployed to monitor individuals in a way that was not possible previously.

Sensitive information collected by drones is particularly vulnerable to unlawful access. In comments addressing the issue of drone test site locations, EPIC observed, "drone hacking," or the process of remotely intercepting and compromising drone operations, poses a threat to the security of lawful drone operations. Recent examples have highlighted the ease with which drones may be "hacked." The University of Texas was able to use GPS signals in order to gain full control of a drone. The researchers indicated that the method could be used on any drone operated over the civilian GPS band, which include the majority of drones in the United States. Hackers are also able to intercept video and audio feeds, as well as other information collected and transmitted by surveillance drones.

Concerns About Customs and Border Protection Drones

Within DHS, the Bureau of Customs and Border Protection ("CBP") is the primary operator of unmanned aerial drones. CBP operates ten drones in the United States, including the Predator B and its maritime variant the Guardian, at a cost per unit of about $18 million each. By 2016, CBP plans to operate twenty-four drones, with the ability to deploy one anywhere in the continental United States within three hours.

But there are problems with the CBP program. According to a recent report of the DHS Inspector General, CBP "needs to improve planning of its unmanned aircraft systems program to address its level of operation, program funding, and resource requirements, along with stakeholder needs." The Inspector General assessed CBP's practice of making the drones available for use by other federal and state agencies, including the Bureau of Land Management, the Department of Defense, the Federal Bureau of Investigation, the Texas Rangers, the United States Forest Service, the National Oceanic and Atmospheric Administration, the Office of Border Patrol, the United States Secret Service, Immigration and Customs Enforcement, the Federal Emergency Management Agency, and local Law Enforcement Agencies.

The Inspector General concluded that all purchases of new drones should be suspended until CBP develops a plan that addresses "necessary operations, maintenance, and equipment." Regarding privacy concerns, the DHS Inspector General said that a standardized process was needed to request CBP drones for non-CBP purposes, in order to "provide transparency."

No legislation currently provides adequate safeguards to protect privacy rights against the increased use of drones in the United States.

Current Privacy Safeguards Are Inadequate

Current regulations permit civil organizations to operate a drone within the United States only pursuant to a special "experimental" designation. However, government operators of drones do not have a similar restriction. Recent policy changes at the FAA, the administrative agency in charge of licensing both governmental and non-governmental drones to operate in the National Airspace, are designed to "streamline" the process by which government agencies, including law enforcement, receive drone licenses.

The CBP currently operates drones with few regulations concerning privacy. No current legislation limits the visual surveillance that a DHS drone may engage in. And while the Privacy Act of 1974 expressly prescribes the circumstances under which agencies can retain personally identifiable information, the Agency may still exempt itself from the Privacy Act provisions that limit the collection and use of personal information. DHS has not sought public comment on or published any specific rules or guidelines that restrict the surveillance practices of its drone program. Also, despite recent releases of records, the FAA's process for the application for and approval of a drone license [is] still mostly opaque, preventing any transparency or accountability for operators.

There are substantial legal and constitutional issues involved in the deployment of aerial drones by federal agencies that need to be addressed. And, as we have noted, no legislation currently provides adequate safeguards to protect privacy rights against the increased use of drones in the United States.

As drone technology becomes cheaper and more proliferate, the threat to privacy will become more substantial. Highrise buildings, security fences, or even the walls of a building are not barriers to increasingly common drone technology.

The Growing Risks

The Supreme Court is aware of the growing risks to privacy resulting from new surveillance technology but has yet to address the specific problems associated with drone surveillance. In *United States v. Jones*, a case that addressed whether the police could use a GPS device to track the movement of a criminal suspect without a warrant, the Court found that the installation and deployment of the device was an unlawful search and seizure. Justice Sotomayor in a concurrence pointed to broader problems associated with new forms of persistent surveillance. And Justice Alito, in a separate concurrence joined by three other Justices, wrote, "in circumstances involving dramatic technological change, the best solution to privacy concerns may be legislative."

As you have indicated, Mister Chairman, the privacy and security concerns arising from the use of drones need to be addressed. Several of your colleagues in the House of Representatives have made efforts to address some of the privacy threats of drones, and we support these initiatives.

An amendment to the National Defense Authorization Act of 2013, introduced by Congressman Jeff Landry (R-LA) and passed by the House, would prohibit information collected by drones operated by the Department of Defense from being used in court as evidence if a warrant was not obtained. In June, House Representative Austin Scott (R-FL) introduced legislation to expand this protection, requiring all law enforcement to first obtain a warrant before conducting any criminal surveillance. Also, Congressman Markey (D-MA) and Congressman Barton (R-TX) sent a letter to the FAA raising concerns about the increased use of Drones in the United States, noting, "there is . . . potential for drone technology to enable invasive and pervasive surveillance without adequate privacy protections."

> *There is no framework in place that ensures that civilian operators and federal agencies . . . utilize drone technology in a privacy-protective manner.*

However, these measures are not sufficient to protect the myriad of privacy interests implicated by increased drone use.

Administrative Action to Address Drone Use

The FAA has been directed by Congress to develop regulations in order to permit more widespread deployment of drones in the United States. The forthcoming regulations will address licensing and procedures for both public and private drone operators, including DHS and CBP. Experts, including Professor Ryan Calo, the former Director of Privacy and Robotics at the Center for Internet and Society at Stanford Law School, have noted that this effort will have significant privacy implications.

Earlier this year, in a formal petition to the agency, EPIC urged the FAA to conduct a privacy rulemaking on the use of drones, with the aim of creating regulations to ensure baseline privacy protections. EPIC's petition was joined by more than one hundred organizations, experts, and members of the public who also believe that drones should not be more widely deployed until privacy safeguards are established.

The FAA has thus far failed to respond to EPIC's request for agency action. The FAA's failure to act means that there is no framework in place that ensures that civilian operators and federal agencies, such as DHS, utilize drone technology in a privacy-protective manner. To the extent that DHS, as well as other agencies, chooses to operate drones within the United States, we believe that the DHS should also develop appropriate regulations to safeguard privacy.

Specifically, the Department of Homeland Security must utilize its Privacy Office, one of the most robust, well-funded Privacy Offices in the federal government. The Privacy Office at DHS "conducts [Privacy Impact Assessments] on technologies, rulemakings, programs, and activities . . . to ensure that privacy considerations and protections are incorporated into all activities of the Department."

However, despite a DHS component operating one of the largest, and definitely the most well publicized drone fleet in the United States for the past seven years, a Privacy Impact Assessment has never been conducted on the privacy impact of drone surveillance. At a minimum, we believe that if the [CBP] plans to continue the drone program, the DHS privacy office must assess the privacy impact of the program and publish a report for public review.

The law should provide for accountability, including third party audits and oversight for federally operated drones and a private right of action against private entities that violate statutory privacy rights.

Safeguards Related to the Use of Drones

There are several strategies to provide meaningful privacy protections that address the increased use of drones in our domestic skies. First, Congress should pass targeted legislation, based on principles of transparency and accountability. A first step would be the consideration and passage of Congressman Scott's bill to limit the use of drone surveillance in criminal investigations without a warrant.

The current state of the law is insufficient to address the drone surveillance threat.

State and local governments have also considered laws and regulations to further prevent abuses of drone technology. These proposals would serve as a good basis for federal legislation. Drone legislation should include:

- Use Limitations—Prohibitions on general surveillance that limit drone surveillance to specific, enumerated circumstances, such as in the case of criminal surveillance subject to a warrant, a geographically-confined emergency, or for reasonable non-law enforcement use where privacy will not be substantially affected;

- Data Retention Limitations—Prohibitions on retaining or sharing surveillance data collected by drones, with emphasis on identifiable images of individuals;

- Transparency—Requiring notice of drone surveillance operations to the extent possible while allowing law enforcement to conduct effective investigations. In addition, requiring notice of all drone surveillance policies through the Administrative Procedure Act.

These three principles would help protect the privacy interests of individuals. In addition, the law should provide for accountability, including third party audits and oversight for federally operated drones and a private right of action against private entities that violate statutory privacy rights.

Second, Congress should act to expressly require federal agencies that choose to operate drones, such as DHS and its components, to implement regulations, subject to public notice and comment, that address the privacy implications of drone use. Recently, in EPIC v. DHS, the D.C. Circuit Court of Appeals ruled that the Department of Homeland Security violated the Administrative Procedure Act when it chose to deploy body scanners as the primary screening technique in U.S. airports without the opportunity for public comment. The Court observed that there was "no justification for having failed to conduct a notice-and-comment rulemaking." We believe that the public has a similar right to comment on new surveillance techniques, such as unmanned aerial vehicles, undertaken by federal agencies within the United States.

Finally, Congress must clarify the circumstances under which the drones purchased by the CBP in pursuit of its mission may be deployed by other agencies for other purposes. The failure to make clear the circumstances when federal and state agencies may deploy drones for aerial surveillance has already raised significant concerns about the agency's program.

The increased use of drones to conduct surveillance in the United States must be accompanied by increased privacy protections. We recognize that drone technology has the potential to be used in positive ways. For example, drones may be used to monitor for environmental abuse, prevent the spread of forest fires, and assist in the rescue of individuals in dangerous situations.

However, the current state of the law is insufficient to address the drone surveillance threat. EPIC supports legislation aimed at strengthening safeguards related to the use of drones as surveillance tools and allowing for redress for drone operators who fail to comply with the mandated standards of protection. We also support compliance with the Administrative Procedure Act for the deployment of drone technology and limitations for federal agencies and other organizations that initially obtain a drone for one purpose and then wish to expand that purpose.

Organizations to Contact

The editors have compiled the following list of organizations concerned with the issues debated in this book. The descriptions are derived from materials provided by the organizations. All have publications or information available for interested readers. The list was compiled on the date of publication of the present volume; names, addresses, phone and fax numbers, and e-mail and Internet addresses may change. Be aware that many organizations take several weeks or longer to respond to inquiries, so allow as much time as possible.

American Security Project (ASP)

1100 New York Ave. NW, Suite 710W, Washington, DC   20005
(202) 347-4267
website: http://americansecurityproject.org

The American Security Project (ASP) believes that America's current national security strategy is flawed, increases worldwide anti-Americanism, and threatens the nation's ability to compete in the global marketplace. The organization hopes to increase public awareness of the true nature of the struggle between the United States and violent extremists so that the nation might develop more effective policies and strategies to meet the threat. On its website ASP publishes issue summaries, recent issues of *American Security Quarterly*, and reports, including *Understanding the Strategies and Tactical Considerations of Drone Strikes*. Under the link Issues/Asymmetric Operations/Strategic Effect of Drones, ASP also publishes an annotated bibliography on drones.

Amnesty International USA

5 Penn Plaza, New York, NY   10001
(212) 807-8400 • fax: (212) 627-1451
e-mail: aimember@aiusa.org
website: www.amnestyusa.org

Amnesty International USA works to ensure that governments do not deny individuals their basic human rights as outlined in the United Nations Universal Declaration of Human Rights. The organization seeks greater transparency in the use of drones and opposes targeted killing without due process. Its website contains recent news, reports, and a searchable database of archived publications, including publications on the impact of drones and drone policy.

Association for Unmanned Vehicle Systems International (AUVSI)

2700 S. Quincy St., Suite 400, Arlington, VA   22206
(703) 845-9671 • fax: (703) 845-9679
e-mail: info@auvsi.org
website: www.auvsi.org

AUVSI is a membership organization that supports unmanned systems and related technology. Members represent government organizations, industry, and academia and support the defense, civil, and commercial sectors. AUVSI publishes the monthly *Unmanned Systems*, which highlights current global developments and unveils new technologies in air, ground, maritime, and space systems.

Brookings Institution

1775 Massachusetts Ave. NW, Washington, DC   20036
(202) 797-6000 • fax: (202) 797-6004
e-mail: brookinfo@brook.edu
website: www.brookings.edu

Founded in 1927, the Brookings Institution conducts research and analyzes global events and their impact on the United States and US foreign policy. It publishes the quarterly *Brookings Review* and numerous books and research papers on foreign policy. Its website publishes editorials, papers, testimony, reports, and articles written by institute scholars, including "The Global Swarm: An International Drone Market," "The Predator Comes Home: A Primer on Domestic Drones, Their

Huge Business Opportunities, and Their Deep Political, Moral, and Legal Challenges," and "When Can the US Target Alleged American Terrorists Overseas?"

Cato Institute

1000 Massachusetts Ave. NW, Washington, DC 20001-5403
(202) 842-0200 • fax: (202) 842-3490
website: www.cato.org

CATO Institute is a libertarian public policy research foundation dedicated to peace and limited government intervention in foreign affairs. It publishes numerous reports and periodicals, including *Policy Analysis* and *Cato Policy Report*, both of which discuss US drone policy as both a domestic and foreign policy tool. Its website contains a searchable database of Institute articles, news, multimedia, and commentary, including the video "Game of Drones: Liberty and Security in the Age of Flying Robots" and the article "Look Up in the Sky and See a Drone."

Center for Security Studies (Georgetown University)

3600 N St. NW, Washington, DC 20007
(202) 687-5679 • fax: (202) 687-5175
website: http://css.georgetown.edu

The Center for Security Studies at Georgetown University studies security issues with the goal of producing a new generation of analysts, policy makers, and scholars fully knowledgeable about the range of international and national security problems and foreign policy issues of the twenty-first century. The Center publishes an online academic review, *Global Security Studies Review (GSSR)*, and a regularly updated weblog, *Global Security Studies Forum*. The website search engine provides links to articles by Center scholars, including "You Say Pakistanis All Hate the Drone War? Prove It."

Center for Strategic and International Studies (CSIS)
1800 K St. NW, Washington, DC   20006
(202) 887-0200 • fax: (202) 755-3199
website: www.csis.org

CSIS conducts research and develops policy recommendations on a variety of issues, including defense and security strategies, economic development, energy and climate change, global health, technology, and trade. The Center publishes *The Washington Quarterly*, recent articles from which are available on its website. CSIS publishes books, reports, newsletters, and commentaries targeted at decision makers in policy, government, business, and academia. Website visitors can access articles on drones through the website's search engine.

Council on Foreign Relations
58 East 68th St., New York, NY   10021
(212) 434-9400 • fax: (212) 434-9800
website: www.cfr.org

The Council on Foreign Relations specializes in foreign affairs and studies the international aspects of American political and economic policies and problems. Its journal *Foreign Affairs*, published five times a year, includes analyses of current conflicts around the world. Its website publishes editorials, interviews, articles, and reports, including the article "Why Did the CIA Stop Torturing and Start Killing?" and the report *Reforming US Drone Strike Policies*.

Human Rights Watch
350 Fifth Ave., 34th Floor, New York, NY   10118-3299
(212) 290-4700 • fax: (212) 736-1300
e-mail: hrwnyc@hrw.org
website: www.hrw.org

Founded in 1978, Human Rights Watch is a nongovernmental organization that conducts systematic investigations of human rights abuses in countries around the world. It publishes many books and reports on specific countries and issues as well as annual reports, recent selections of which are available on its website. Publications on drones include "What Rules Should Govern US Drone Attacks?," "A Dangerous Model: The US Should Reveal Its Legal Rationale for Drone Attacks," and "Anatomy of an Air Attack Gone Wrong."

New America Foundation

1899 L St. NW, Suite 400, Washington, DC   20036
(202) 986-2700 • fax: (202) 986-3696
website: www.newamerica.net

The New America Foundation invests in new thinkers and new ideas to address the next generation of challenges facing the United States. New America emphasizes research that responds to the changing conditions and problems of the twenty-first century information-age economy. The website provides links to books by Foundation authors. Also on its website, the Foundation provides access to articles, blogs, and policy papers, including "Revenge of the Drones" and "The Year of the Drone" study, an analysis of US drone strikes in Pakistan from 2004 to 2013.

The Rutherford Institute

PO Box 7482, Charlottesville, VA   22966-7482
(434) 978-3888
e-mail: staff@rutherford.org
website: www.rutherford.org

The Rutherford Institute is a conservative civil liberties think tank with a dual mission. It provides legal services in the defense of religious and civil liberties and seeks to educate the public on important issues affecting constitutional freedoms. The Institute supports strong civil liberties protections from constitutional invasions by domestic drones. Its website publishes news and commentary on the domestic use of drones, including "Roaches, Mosquitoes, and Birds: The Coming Micro-Drone Revolution" and commentary by its founder, constitutional attorney John W. Whitehead.

Bibliography

Books

Michael Barnes and Florian Jentsch, eds. *Human-Robot Interactions in Future Military Operations.* Burlington, VT: Ashgate, 2010.

Shahzad Bashir and Robert D. Crews, eds. *Under the Drones: Modern Lives in the Afghanistan Pakistan Borderlands.* Cambridge, MA: Harvard University Press, 2012.

Medea Benjamin *Drone Warfare: Killing by Remote Control.* New York: W.W. Norton, 2013.

Christopher Coker *Ethics and War in the 21st Century.* New York: Routledge, 2009.

Lydia de Beer, ed. *Unmanned Aircraft Systems (Drones) and Law.* Nijmegen, The Netherlands: Wolf Legal Publishers, 2011.

Charles Guthrie and Michael Quinlan *Just War: The Just War Tradition, Ethics in Modern Warfare.* New York: Walker & Company, 2009.

Armin Krishnan *Killer Robots: Legality and Ethicality of Autonomous Weapons.* Burlington, VT: Ashgate, 2009.

Matt J. Martin and Charles W. Sasser *Predator: The Remote-Control Air War over Iraq and Afghanistan, a Pilot's Story.* Minneapolis, MN: Zenith Press, 2010.

Peter W. Singer   *Wired for War: The Robotics Revolution and Conflict in the 21st Century*. New York: Penguin, 2009.

Brian Glyn Williams   *Predators: The CIA's Drone War on al Qaeda*. Dulles, VA: Potomac Books, 2013.

Periodicals and Internet Sources

Kenneth Anderson   "Predators over Pakistan," *Weekly Standard*, March 6, 2010.

Randal C. Archibold   "US Adds Drones to Fight Smuggling," *New York Times*, December 8, 2009.

Lolita C. Baldor   "Legal Questions Raised over CIA Drone Strikes," *Boston Globe*, April 29, 2010.

Julian E. Barnes   "US Crews Retrain for Drone Battle," *Los Angeles Times*, March 29, 2010.

Peter Bergen and Katherine Tiedemann   "The Year of the Drone: An Analysis of US Drone Strikes in Pakistan, 2004–2010," New American Foundation, February 24, 2010. www.newamerica.net.

Thomas J. Billitteri   "Drone Warfare," *CQ Researcher*, August 6, 2010.

Gail Chatfield   "Domestic Drones a Threat," *North County Times (San Diego)*, September 10, 2012.

Ed Collins	"Drones, Terrorists, & the Ethics of War," *Ethics Newsline*, July 16, 2012. www.globalethics.org.
Adam Entous	"Special Report: How the White House Learned to Love the Drone," Reuters, May 18, 2010. www.reuters.com.
C. Christine Fair	"Drone Wars," *Foreign Policy*, May 28, 2010.
Peter Finn	"US Urged to Stop CIA Drone Hits in Pakistan," *Washington Post*, June 3, 2010.
Siobhan Gorman, Yochi J. Dreazen, and August Cole	"Insurgents Hack US Drones," *Wall Street Journal*, December 17, 2009.
Shane Harris	"Are Drone Strikes Murder?," *National Journal*, January 9, 2010.
Greg Jaffe	"Drone Pilots Rise on Wings of Change in Air Force," *Washington Post*, February 28, 2010.
James Joyner	"America's Scandalous Drone War Goes Unmentioned in the Campaign," *New Republic*, September 26, 2012.
John Kaag and Sarah Kreps	"The Moral Hazard of Drones," *New York Times*, July 22, 2012.
Charles G. Kels	"Drones Kill Transnational Terrorists," *Washington Times*, July 31, 2012.

Sarah Kreps and John Kaag — "The Use of Unmanned Aerial Vehicles in Contemporary Conflicts: A Legal and Ethical Analysis," *Polity*, 2012.

Gregory M. Lamb — "New Role for Robot Warriors," *Christian Science Monitor*, February 17, 2010.

Michael W. Lewis — "Drones and the Boundaries of the Battlefield," *Texas International Law Journal*, Spring 2012.

Rich Lowry — "The Great Drone Panic," *National Review*, July 6, 2012.

Jane Mayer — "The Predator War," *New Yorker*, October 26, 2009.

Rand Paul — "Don't Let Drones Invade Our Privacy," CNN.com, June 15, 2012. www.cnn.com.

Sheldon Richman — "America's Drone Terrorism," *New American*, October 19, 2012.

Eugene Robinson — "The Emerging 'Drone' Culture," *Miami Herald*, August 6, 2012.

Charlie Savage — "UN Report Highly Critical of US Drone Attacks," *New York Times*, June 2, 2010.

Scott Shane — "The Moral Case for Drones," *New York Times*, July 14, 2012.

John Villasenor — "Will Drones Outflank the Fourth Amendment?," *Forbes*, September 20, 2012. www.forbes.com.

Index

A

ABC News poll, 10
Administrative Procedure Act,
    108–110
Afghanistan
    drone attacks in, 44, 56, 64,
        90
    due process and, 23
    Predator drones in, 8, 15
    US military force in, 10, 46,
        47
Agile Falcon demonstration, 78
Air and Marine Operations Center
    (AMOC), 78, 80, 82
Alienation of allies, 30–32
al Qaeda
    as drone targets, 9–10, 12, 14,
        25, 56
    Muslim support, 51
    nonintervention standards
        and, 59
    recruits in, 17
    terrorist recruitment by, 62
    US armed conflict with, 47,
        53–54
    war on, 48, 49
    in Yemen, 31
Al Qaeda in the Arabian Peninsula
    (AQAP), 32–33
America Magazine, 56–59
American Civil Liberties Union
    (ACLU), 95
Ansar al-Sharia, 32
Anti-Americanism, 31, 36
Anti-drone rallies, 36
Army Corps of Engineers, 77

Association for Unmanned Ve-
    hicles Systems International
    (AUVSI), 96
Automated license plate readers,
    101
Automatic information system
    (AIS), 79

B

Battlefield restraints with drones,
    49–51
Belew, Lyle, 87
Bennett, Brian, 84–88
bin Laden, Osama, 7, 17, 61
Black, Hector, 87–88
Black Hawk missiles, 70
Bolivia, 58
Bonner, T.J., 86
Border patrol by drones
    advantages of, 70–72
    authorizations for, 78–79
    challenges with, 82–83
    concerns over, 103–104
    cooperative operations, 77–78
    effectiveness of, 74–83
    enhancing homeland security
        with, 81–82
    example of, 84–85
    future plans, 80–81
    Guardian Unmanned Aircraft
        System, 74–75, 79, 83
    maritime domain and, 79–80
    mixed results from, 85–86
    overview, 74–75
    pros and cons, 87–88
    record as unimpressive, 86–87

strategy for, 75–77
as unproven, 84–88
Boumediene v. Bush, 22
Brazil, 58
Brennan, John O., 9–10
Brown, George S., 7
Bureau of Land Management, 103
Bush, George W. (administration),
13, 26, 47, 61

C

Calo, Ryan, 106
Canada, 47, 70
Center for Internet and Society,
106
Central Intelligence Agency (CIA)
countervailing check of, 19–20
drone use by, 7–10, 13–14
drones as targeting, 12, 17–19
Inspector General of, 21
rules of engagement by, 15
Certificates of Authorization
(COAs), 78–81
Clinton, Bill (administration), 61
Cocaine trafficking, 86
Congressional Unmanned Systems
Caucus, 72
Counter-terrorism operations, 51,
57

D

Data retention limitations for
drones, 108
Deepwater Horizon oil spill, 79
Dragon Eye drones, 7
Drones
anti-drone rallies, 36

environmental protection by,
89–93
international laws for, 56–59
introductions, 7–11
overview, 12–13, 56
sovereignty and noninterference, 58–59
See also Environmental protection by drones; Piloting of
drones
Drones, domestic use
administrative actions to address, 106–107
as border patrol, 70–72, 74–
83, 103–104
as civil liberty threat, 63–67
concerns over, 69–70
criticism of, 69
legal safeguards needed, 100–
110
overview, 63–64, 68–69, 100–
101
potential for, 64–65
privacy safeguards, 104–105,
107–110
privacy threat from, 101–103
risks in, 105–106
technology advances in, 65–66
weaponizing of, 66–67
Drones, law enforcement
battlefield definition in, 47–48
battlefield restraints, 49–51
battlefield weapons and,
44–45
improper use of, 45–47
overview, 43–44
should not be used, 43–51
terrorist status and, 48–49
Drones, targeting with
balance in, 20–21
certainty over, 16–19
control of, 14–16

as legal and effective, 12–23
legal objections to, 22–23
limits and standards, 13–14
military model of, 19–20
precaution over, 18–19
problems with, 57–58
reasonable doubt and, 14–16
tempering power of, 21–22
Drones, terrorism
alienating allies, 30–32
allure of, 25
controversy over, 9–10
counter-terrorism operations,
51
extrajudicial killing, 26
extremism and, 33
government tyranny in, 21–22
as harmful and ineffective,
24–29
impact of, 61–62
overview, 24–25, 30
as promotion of terrorism,
30–33
public debate of, 60–62
role of, 60–61
the rule of law, 27–28
terrorist recruiting and, 32–33
US hatred increases, 28–29
Due process concerns, 57–58

E

Electronic Privacy Information
Center (EPIC), 100–102, 106–
107
El mosco (Predator drone), 84
Environmental Protection Agency,
70
Environmental protection by
drones
as effective tool, 89–93
efficiency of, 92

other tools, 92–93
overview, 89–90
usefulness of, 90–91
EPIC v. DHS, 109
Error of judgment in drone tar-
geting, 20
Ethiopia, 46
Extra-judicial assassination, 13, 26
Extremism and drone strikes, 33
Exum, Andrew, 8

F

Facial recognition technology, 102
Federal Aviation Administration
(FAA)
basing agreements, 81
drone licenses, 104–105
drone regulation by, 101, 106–
107
flying rights, 64, 69
national air space for drones,
78–79, 82–83, 95
need for, 99
Federal Bureau of Investigation
(FBI), 102, 103
Federal Emergency Management
Agency (FEMA), 76–77, 103
Firebombing, 39
Flash-Ball gun, 67
France, 47
Franklin, Percival, 90, 92

G

Gates, Robert, 64
General Atomics, 8
Geneva Conventions, 53–54
Germany, 47
Global Hawk drones, 7

Gnat drones, 7
Government Accountability Office (GAO), 70
GPS sensors, 101
Gray, Denis D., 89–93
Greenwood, Christopher, 48
Grenier, Robert, 30–31
Guardian Unmanned Aircraft System (UAS), 74–75, 79, 83

H

Hacker concerns, 103
Hambling, David, 67
Harvard Law School, 10
Hearing damage, 66
Heat sensors, 101
Hellfire missiles, 8, 25, 45
High-intensity strobe lights, 66
Holder, Eric, 10, 26
Hussein, Saddam, 44
Hydrogen bomb, 40

I

Iannotta, Ben, 60–62
IDENT database, 102
Immigration and Customs Enforcement, 103
India, 28
Indonesia, 47, 90
Industry code of conduct
    backlash of, 96–97
    consequences and, 97–98
    controversy over, 98–99
    as inadequate, 94–99
    overview, 94–95
    public relations nightmare, 95–96
Infrared cameras, 101

Inspector General of CIA, 21
International Committee of the Red Cross, 49, 50
International Court of Justice, 48
International humanitarian law (IHL), 13, 14, 17, 23, 57
International Law Association's Committee on the Use of Force, 47
Iraq, 46, 64
Iraq War, 57
Israel, 27

J

Jihadists, 28

K

Kaag, John, 38–42
Kels, Charles G., 52–55
Khan, Imran, 24–25
Kilcullen, David, 51
Klaidman, Daniel, 56
Koh, Harold, 16–17, 47
Koh, Lian Pin, 90–91
Kostelnik, Michael C., 74–83, 86–87
Krauthammer, Charles, 61–62, 69, 95
Kreps, Sarah, 38–42

L

Landry, Jeff, 105
Law of Armed Conflict, 57
Lin, Jeffrey, 94–99
Long Range Acoustic Devices (LRADs), 66

Los Angeles County Sheriff's Department, 65

M

Madison, James, 63
Malaysia, 91
Marijuana trafficking, 85, 86
Meyer, John C., 7
Military model of drones targeting, 19–20
Moral questions
overview, 38–39
reasons for, 39–40
technology and, 40–42
in warfare, 38–42
Morocco, 47
Mothana, Ibrahim, 30–33
Mutual assured destruction (MAD), 40

N

Nadim, Hussain, 34–37
National Aeronautics and Space Administration (NASA), 8, 83
National Air Security Operations Office (NASO), 76
National Airspace System (NAS), 75, 78–79, 82–83
National Border Patrol Council, 86
National Defense Authorization Act (2013), 105
National Oceanic and Atmospheric Administration, 103
National Public Radio Report, 51
Native American Choctaw nation, 8
Navy Global Hawk drone, 68–69

Necessity principle, 49
Nepal, 90, 91
New America Foundation, 9, 25
New York Air National Guard, 77–78
New York Times (newspaper), 13, 51
New York University, 27
Next Generation Identification database, 102
Noninterference concerns, 58–59
North Dakota Air National Guard, 77
Northwestern University Law School, 10
Nuclear holocaust, 39
Nuclear weapons, 40, 87

O

Obama Barack (administration)
access to classified memos, 9–10
deaths by drones under, 26
drone strikes authorized by, 31, 51, 56
drones as targeting tools, 13, 18, 20, 22
self-defense justifications, 58
O'Connell, Mary Ellen, 43–51
Office of Air and Marine (OAM), 75
Office of Border Patrol, 103
Office of Legal Counsel, 18

P

P-3 Orion maritime surveillance planes, 70, 80, 82
Pakistan
drone attacks in, 56, 90

drone deaths in, 39
drone use in, 9, 34–37, 49–51
hatred of, 28
sovereignty of, 27
Pakistan People's Party, 36
Paul, Rand, 68–69
Peterson, Scott, 84–85
Piloting of drones
    critics of, 53–54
    not violation of international
        law, 52–55
    overview, 9, 14–16, 52
    uniform requirements, 54–55
Powers, Francis Gary, 7
Predator drones
    for border patrol, 70–71, 74–
        77, 80, 84–86
    domestic use of, 20
    naming of, 7–8
    purchase of by DHS, 86
    against terrorism, 25
Predator Ops center, 87
Preserving Freedom from Unwar-
    ranted Surveillance Act, 68–69
Prisoners of war (POWs), 53–54
PrisonPlanet.com, 67
Privacy Act (1974), 104
Privacy safeguards for drones,
    104–105, 107–110
Proportionality principle, 49
Protocol I, Geneva Conventions,
    53

R

Radicalization in Pakistan, 35
Radsan, Afsheen John, 12–23
Reagan, Ronald, 48–49
Reaper drones, 8, 25
Reasonable doubt in drone usage,
    14–16

Relevant factors in drone target-
    ing, 20
Roosevelt, Franklin D., 40
Rubber pellet usage, 67
The rule of law, 27–28, 51
Rules of engagement (ROEs), 15

S

Sanger, David E., 56
Saudi Arabia, 47
Scott, Austin, 105, 108
Sea Shepherd Conservation Soci-
    ety, 90
Second Amendment, 95
September 11, 2001, attacks, 25,
    69
al-Shabwani, Jabir, 31
Shahzad, Faisal, 28
Singer, Peter W., 94–99
SkySeer drone, 65
Somalia, 46, 56
Sound cannons, 64
Sovereignty concerns, 58–59
Soviet Union, 7, 40
Spain, 47
Special rapporteurs (UN), 28
Stanford Law School, 106
Stanford University, 27
Stepanovich, Amie, 100–110
Stinger missiles, 35
Strategic Air and Marine Plan
    (StAMP), 80
Strategic Air Command, 7
Sumatra, 92
Sumatran Orangutan Conserva-
    tion Program, 90
Swiss Federal Institute of Technol-
    ogy, 90

T

Taliban
  as drone targets, 12, 25
  radicalization by, 35
  recruits in, 17
  US armed conflict with, 47
Taser usage, 64, 66–67
Taylor, Telford, 54
Tear gas usage, 64, 66
Tecknisolar Seni, 67
Texas Rangers, 103
Thailand, 92–93
Thakur, Ramesh, 24–29
Thermonuclear conflagration, 40
Times Square bomber, 28
Transparency for drones, 108
Truman, Harry S., 40, 41

U

U-2 spy plane, 7
UAS Maritime Demonstration, 79
Ugalla Primate Project, 91
Ultralight craft, 92–93
Undocumented immigrants, 72
Uniform Code of Military Justice, 50
United Kingdom (UK), 47, 49
United Nations Basic Principles for the Use of Force and Firearms by Law Enforcement Officials, 44–45
United Nations Charter, 53
United Nations Commission on Human Rights, 45
United States Air Force (USAF), 7, 25
United States Coast Guard (USCG), 75, 76, 77
United States Forest Service, 103
United States Secret Service, 103
United States v. Jones, 105
University of Florida, 90, 92
University of Maryland, 65
University of Texas, 103
Unmanned aerial vehicles (UAVs). *See* Drones
US Constitution, 26
US Customs and Border Protection (CBP)
  drone use by, 8, 68–72, 75–83
  drug trafficking, 84–85
  primary domestic drone operator, 103–104
  role of, 75
US Department of Defense (DOD)
  border protection concerns, 103
  collateral damage procedures, 18
  drone fleet, 11, 72
  evidence in court, 105
  homeland security by, 81–82
  targeted killing role, 13
US Department of Homeland Security (DHS)
  drone regulation by, 107
  drone use by, 68, 74, 76, 85–86, 102
  drone violation by, 109
  enhancing missions by, 81–82
US Justice Department, 18
Use limitations for drones, 108
Usher, Graham, 91
Uzbekistan, 44

W

Washington Post (newspaper), 10, 61
Wasp drones, 7
Watson, Paul Joseph, 67
Weaponizing domestic drones, 66–67
Whitehead, John W., 63–67
Wich, Serge, 91
Wired News (online news site), 67
World War II, 23
World Wide Fund for Nature (WWF), 91
Wyden, Ron, 9–10

Y

Yemen
 drone attacks in, 56, 61
 drone deaths in, 45–46
 drone opposition by, 9, 32–33
 drones as targeting tools, 13
 terrorism in, 47
 US hatred by, 30–31

Z

Zenko, Micah, 68–73